LIVING WITH

FINANCIAL ANXIETY

Leibel Sternbach

Printed in the United States of America

Print ISBN: 978-1-63901-350-0
E-Book ISBN: 978-1-63901-351-7

For more information, email: hello@leibelsternbach.com

LIVING WITH
FINANCIAL
ANXIETY

will match or exceed any particular benchmark. All investment strategies have the potential for profit or loss. Asset allocation and diversification do not ensure or guarantee better performance and cannot eliminate the risk of investment losses.

Projections are based on assumptions that may not come to pass. They do not reflect the impact that advisory fees and other investment-related expenses will have on the value of an investor's portfolio.

All insurance products are subject to the claims-paying ability of the insurer.

Not an offer to solicit investment advice of financial services. Please contact a licensed CPA, Attorney, or financial advisor before implementing any of the advice in this book. The opinions in this book are solely the reflection of the author and do not represent Fusion Capital Management.

CONTENTS

Introduction

LIVING WITH FINANCIAL ANXIETY

I NITIALLY, I WAS GOING to call this book "The 5 Minute Financial Plan." After writing the book, I realized that this isn't a plan, so much as the anti-planning process. Financial Planning doesn't work!

In today's, fast paced, ever evolving digital landscape, taking months, weeks, or even days to plan out a decision, is just not feasible. Yet, the cost of failure has never been so high. Social safety nets are slowly deteriorating, and the cost of failure is growing higher.

In this book, I will share with you a process that I have been using in my life. It is a process that I have used for as long as I can remember, I didn't even realize it was "my process." I just thought this was how everyone approached decision making. This process takes less than five minutes, it is a process that aligns your life and your finances. It is a way of making decisions that remove financial anxieties and helps you achieve your dreams faster.

This book is written for my friends, my family and everyone for whom financial anxiety is a daily part of their lives. In this book, you will find the simple answers that will transform your relationship with money and keep you on the path for financial success.

Traditional financial planning does not work! As human beings, we are emotional creatures. We make decisions for emotional reasons. We do not stay up at night wondering if our plants are going to grow. We worry at night: "did we turn off the stove," or "did we lock the door." Traditional financial plans will always fail, because they address the financial needs, without acknowledging, and incorporating their emotional context.

In this book, you will discover a simple and revolutionary process for personal financial freedom. It is a process that is based on my experience working with hundreds of amazing advisors, teachers, and businessmen.

Living with Financial Anxiety is the culmination of the wisdom of hundreds of advisors, broken down into bite sized pieces that you can implement in your life today.

Financial freedom is yours for the taking! You just need to be bold enough to take it! Discover how to live the life of your dreams without financial worry of anxiety.

Chapter 1

BUYING HAPPINESS

PEOPLE WOULD HAVE YOU believe that money does not buy happiness. They will tell you that happiness comes from within, they will tell you that happiness comes from being happy with what you have. Of course, those people have never gone a day without food, they have not worried about paying their rent, or skimped on life-saving medicine because they could not afford it. Not only have I done all those things, and many more; I am here to tell you that money and happiness are very much intertwined.

In fact, I personally think, this obsession with downplaying the importance of money, is one of the biggest reasons why people are anxious and unhappy.

The world is filled with myths, misconceptions, and "conventional wisdom" that are inaccurate or downright lies. These are lies people have been telling themselves for generations, either because they were once true and no longer apply, or because "everyone" perpetuates them. These myths will hurt your financial wellbeing and your happiness.

Financial security and happiness is something we can all achieve. In this book, I am going to teach you everything you need to know, to take control of your financial future and ensure your dreams come true.

The Source of Money Anxiety

The biggest source of anxiety, for most people, is a fear of the unknown. When we look at our financial world, it is a great big unknown. We do not know what the future holds. We can only guess at how much money we will need in retirement, or how our savings will do. Or we may worry about our car breaking down, a pipe bursting in our home, or any number of other financial emergencies that may come up. It is this fear of the unknown and its potential consequences that keep us up at night. It is why we stay in jobs we do not like; it is why we say "yes" to clients we hate. Fear is why we avoid talking to our partner about money, and our feelings towards money.

If only we had a crystal ball, we would know for sure how things will turn out and what to do.

While we may not have a crystal ball, we can protect ourselves financially from the unknown. The more we insulate ourselves from the chaos of life and the unknown, the more we can take control of our happiness.

There are studies that have been conducted regarding stress and money. Universally, these studies have found that when people do not have enough money or they stress about the money, they make poor financial decisions. Is it that these people are making poor decisions, or is it that they do not have the same options that are available to everyone else?

In nature, when food is scarce, the body tends to build up its fat reserves, preserving energy for the future. Money seems to work the opposite, when money is scarce, we tend to make short-term decisions rather than long-term decisions. At least according to the research that seems to be what is happening. The issue with studies of this nature is that the researchers have never gone hungry, they have never run up credit card debt, or been evicted.

The short-term decisions that people make with money are very much in line with human nature. In essence, we are converting our material possessions to satisfy our immediate needs for food and shelter; since biologically we do not know if there will be a tomorrow. What is the purpose of saving for tomorrow if it never comes?

Fundamentally, this dichotomy is probably the biggest obstacle to one's financial success. Our bodies urge us, physically and emotionally, in one direction, but economics requires us to move differently, which causes us great distress. Compounding the problem, the world is filled with people shouting generic advice that may, or may not be, right for us, in our particular situation.

Taking Back Control

As a human being, the only way to take back control of your happiness, is to take control of your financial future, and leverage your biological urges rather than fight against nature.

Living with Anxiety is my answer to this problem. In this book, I discuss my 5-minute financial planning process, a process that leverages our emotions, and human nature, to enable us to make financial decisions, each and every time. By the end of this book, you will feel confident in your ability to make the best financial decision for yourself and your loved ones. The goal is that financial anxiety will be a thing of the past, and you will be able to focus on enjoying the fruits of your labor.

The chapters in this book are designed to be bite-sized, and help you take specific steps on your journey to financial freedom. Before you know, you will have transformed from a layperson, anxious and afraid, to someone ready to take life by the horns, unafraid of what the future might bring, because you know that you have the tools to overcome any financial obstacle.

The biggest challenge to financial freedom is stress. The stress of: not knowing where our next meal is coming from, of not having a roof over our heads, of being rejected by our friends, family, peers, or community.

The easiest way to relieve this stress is to remove the stress entirely. The only way to remove this stress is by removing the cause of our stress - which is a lack of money.

If we lose our job, we lose our source of income, which means, we may not be able to put a roof over our head or food on our tables. If our car breaks down, we may not be able to fix it and go to work. the list of possible stressors is endless.

Regardless of your wealth or station in life, you will always find these stressors. Wealth only transforms the object of your stress. In the beginning, your stress may be "not being able to put food on your table," then it might be "not having a big enough house," or "a lavish enough vacation."

You might be thinking to yourself; I live in a shoebox; I would never stress about not having a big enough house!

So did I, until it happened to me. I am the oldest of 7 siblings, I grew up in a one-bedroom apartment, we lived in the proverbial shoebox. Recently, me, my wife and kid (3 people) moved from a 1600 sq foot house to a 3300 sq foot house - because our small house was causing stress and marital strife.

As we go through life, our needs and stressors change, what gives us comfort becomes the source of our future anxieties. As we grow and adapt, our toolsets need to grow and adapt as well.

My purpose in telling you all this is because, regardless of where you are in life, the fundamentals will always remain the same, it is the implementation that will change.

Combating Financial Anxiety

How do we relieve financial anxiety? By removing the stress entirely!

Take a few moments and define your fears? Is it that you are afraid of not being able to pay your mortgage or bills? is it the fear of your car breaking down? Or maybe you are like my sister-in-law, who lives in a 10,000 sq foot house, but fears her appliances breaking? Whatever your financial fears are, write them down, give them life, define them. Once you have them defined, then we can overcome them!

The next step is to ask yourself, what would relieve your anxiety?

If you had a magic wand that gave you a year's worth of free rent, would that be enough? The answer is different for everyone. It is easy to cop out and say, "What do the experts think?" The experts are not you; they do not live in your body; they do not know how you feel...and they certainly are not going to be staying up with you in the middle of the night, when you are anxious.

Be honest with yourself and ask yourself what it would take for you to no longer be financially worried?

If you are having trouble, one way you can approach this exercise is to walk through your worst financial fears. Think through what that might be. My wife has irrational anxiety about running out of money, for her it isn't just about paying the mortgage or having food on the table, it's a bottomless and amorphous fear.

An exercise we do together is to talk through and discuss what would happen if we both lost our jobs. We walk through what our savings would look like if we lived our current lifestyle without any changes, we also talk about the types of things we could or couldn't change and still be ok. For my wife, having a yearly vacation is really, really important, as such it is part of our "emergency fund" planning.

What are the things that are important to you? What are the things that you **could** live without? How might your life change in a worst-case scenario? What are the things you could NOT live without?

There are no right or wrong answers. There were a few times in my life where I was an alcoholic. On one such occasion, I vividly remember walking to the grocery store to buy myself dinner. I did not have food in the fridge, halfway to the grocery store, I got a craving for cigarettes and scotch. Long story short, I didn't have dinner that night. At the time cigarettes and scotch were more important to me than food - or getting my car fixed. Was it a smart financial decision? Was it the right decision? It does not really matter - it was the decision I could live with at the time.

Financial planning is not for the high points in your life, it is for the low points. It is to help prevent you, or your loved ones, from having to decide which of their needs are greater.

Creating Your Freedom Fund

Once you know what your bottom line is, your next step is to quantify it financially and solve for it.

In the financial planning vernacular, this is known as an "emergency fund", or the way I like to think of it, it is an FU fund.

I think of it as the FU fund, because it is what gives you the emotional strength to be able to say "NO!" Your FU fund, is what allows you to live a life without regret. It allows you to remove the financial anxiety from life because you know that no matter what happens in life, you have the financial ability to withstand it, and come through it stronger and better than before.

Once you have a FU fund, financial decisions no longer have the same "fight or flight" hold on you. This allows you to take the time to think through your decisions and make the best decisions for yourself and your loved ones. No longer will you feel pressured to make decisions on someone else's schedule, because after all, you know that no matter what happens you will be OK.

Your "Emergency Fund" or "FU" fund is really your financial freedom fund. It is your key to financial happiness and a better life.

Sources of Emergency Funds

Once you have emotionally determined the requirements for your emergency fund, the next step is to decide how we are going to fund it. The key requirement for your emergency fund is that it needs to be relatively stable. You don't want to be worrying about your fund disappearing overnight, in a market crash. You also want to have access to your funds quickly in an emergency. Some common sources for Emergency Funds are:

1. Savings Accounts
2. Credit Cards
3. Home Equity Line of Credit (HELOC)
4. Life insurance policies that have loan provisions
5. Supplemental Insurance
6. Bank CDs

Savings accounts are the traditional source of emergency funds. Credit cards and lines of credit can be great sources of funds; however, I would caution you not to be overly reliant on them, since credit lines can often disappear or shrink when you need them the most. I learned this lesson the hard way during the great recession, when I had my credit card limits lowered every single month!

Another option, life insurance policies with loan provisions, which are usually set up as low-interest loans from a cash value policy. Ideally, you want to save that money for retirement. However, if you need to tap into emergency cash, you can consider your life insurance policy, in essence it is a secured loan that uses your policy as collateral.

You may be tempted to include your home equity as part of your "emergency fund." I would caution against it. In addition to the time and cost of obtaining funds against your home equity, chances are that any event that requires those types of funds will also disqualify you from a traditional bank loan.

One last note: I highly recommend opening a separate savings account for your emergency fund. Personally, I like having mine at a separate bank that is far from my home. I don't even have a debit card for this account. This helps me avoid the temptation to use it when I shouldn't. I also recommend funding your emergency funds with automatic debits from your paycheck. The amount you put away is less important than the regular stocking/re-stocking of your account. A small amount, untouched and saved each month, will accumulate quickly over time.

Chapter 2

BECOMING LUCKY

HAVE YOU EVER NOTICED how some people seem to catch all the breaks, make every green light and things just seem to go their way? Have you ever wondered what makes those people lucky while others constantly struggle to survive?

One of the best kept secrets of Wall Street is that successful investors manufacture luck. Successful people work around the clock each day to create their own luck and they are always increasing their luck surface area.

The more luck you have the more likely your dreams are to become a reality.

In this chapter we are going to cover how you can manufacture your own luck and shift the tides of life in your favor. We are going to discuss the different types of luck, how to increase your luck surface area, and how to diversify your luck so that the chances of accomplishing your life goals increases.

What Is Luck

A better word to use for Luck is realized opportunities. The Oxford dictionary defines an opportunity as "a set of circumstances that makes it possible to do something."

Opportunities are everywhere when you know how to look. By visualizing goals, opportunities are noticed and acted on.

Visualization, is the act of imagining a future success or event, as if it were happening now. As Aristotle writes, "We become what we think." In a way, by visualizing your dreams, you can in fact help manifest them into reality.

Of course, visualization is not enough, one needs to act. It may not be easy, but it is possible with a little hard work and determination to achieve all your goals in life.

Determine Your Goals

The first step, it articulate for yourself, in detail, your life goals. As the Cheshire Cat says to Alice in Wonderland "if you don't know where you are going, any road will take you there." This is the case in life, if we do not know what our goals are then it will be difficult to achieve them. There must first come awareness of your desires and intentions before any other steps can begin.

Think to yourself, what do you want your future to look like? Where do you want to live? What do you want your lifestyle to be? What are the important features?

The first time I *really* did this exercise, I was 17 years old, I took a few days and visualized for myself possible futures. What I discovered was that the things that were important to me in life, were being around when my future kids when they are young, watching them grow up, and being able to control my work schedule.

What are the things that are important to you? Do you want a house with a pool? Or to be debt free? Or travel without worrying about the cost? Do you want to be able to take a cruise once a year? Take the time to really think about what it is that you want from life, and why you want those things?

The more you understand the why behind your wants, the better positioned you will be to realize your goals. Life rarely turns out the way we expect. The more you understand the why behind your goals, the more likely you are to be to be able to recognize when life presents opportunities that will help you further your goals or move you away from your goals.

The more opportunities you can recognize, the better you will be able to take action that will lead you closer to your dreams.

Life Rarely Turns Out the Way We Expect

As a kid, a common story that my teachers would tell us was about a man who was drowning. The man is struggling to stay afloat, praying to God to save him. This is a man of utmost faith, and he knows without a doubt that God will save him.

As he is struggling in the water praying, a rescue helicopter comes by and lowers to him a lifesaver, the man refuses, saying "God will save me." A little while longer a boat comes along and offers to rescue him, the man refuses, saying "God will save me." Long story short the man drowns, when he comes to heaven, he rails against God, "how could you not save me? I was a pious man, a religious man, I did everything right, why didn't you save me!?" God replies that he sent the helicopter and the boat to save him.

Life rarely turns out the way we expect it. It is easy to get caught up in the specifics. It is easy to miss the opportunities that were and are available. The opportunities that could have given us the lifestyle we wanted. It may not have been exactly how we imagined, and I can virtually guarantee you that it won't be how you imagine, but it will have enough of the characteristics that are important to you - if you are honest with yourself and open to life.

This philosophy goes against everything that we are taught about goals. We are taught that goals should be **SMART**; **Specific, M**easurable, **A**chievable, **R**ealistic and **T**imely. Your life goals should be none of these things. They should be general in nature, as such they aren't really measurable.

Since these are major life goals, ideally, they should be things that seem a little out of reach, maybe a little unrealistic (at least right now.) I don't know about you, but I have a very hard time controlling life. Who could have predicted COVID? Tying yourself to specific timelines seems like a surefire recipe for disappointment.

We are emotional creatures; the feeling and experience of our end goal is more important than the specifics. If we want to live by the beach, does it matter which town? What type of house? No! All that matters is that we get that emotional contentment that comes with being near and experiences of, living by the beach.

What about specific goals, like paying for college? Or buying a house?

It may be tempting to cop out and say these rules don't apply to me, or to my goal. You might say to yourself "I have a very specific goal, I need $10k for X." While having a specific goal is commendable. If you become overly focused on the specifics, you may miss out on the other opportunities that life presents to you to achieve your ultimate life goals. For instance, if you are saving for your kids or grandkids college expenses, you may become so focused on a specific number that you entirely miss the opportunity for them to get a free scholarship, or grants, etc.... As we will discuss later, you do need to take action to achieve your goal, but you don't want to be married to specific paths.

Increasing Your Luck Surface Area

Once you have a good idea of what your life goals are, the next step is to map out the milestones for your goal. What are the things that need to happen in order for you to achieve your goal(s)?

Let us take something simple, like buying a home. To buy a home, you need to have a means to buy a home, either cash on hand or a stable job and credit for getting a mortgage. You need to have an idea of what type of home you want to own, what are the aspects of a home that are important to you? For me, I like to cook, and I work from home, having a good kitchen and a room for a home office is critical. Do you need a down payment? How much of a down payment will you need?

You define the steps and the details that are important. By taking action along the path to accomplishing your goals, open yourself up to new possibilities.

A perfect example, my wife wanted a bigger home. She had determined that she wanted a house with a bigger yard, and we had determined what our ideal price range was. We weren't "active" buyers, but we had discussions, we talked in general terms to mortgage brokers, and every now and then we would look online at available houses. Occasionally we would go to open houses. Buying a new house was something that we knew we would eventually have to do, but it was not something that was time sensitive.

One day we were out walking, and we saw a for sale sign go up on a property. It was a much smaller house than ours, smaller than anything we were looking for, but it was on a large piece of property. My wife called up the seller, long story short, a year and half later we were living in our custom-built home. Due to the oddities of the housing market at the time, the cost to build a new house was similar to purchasing the type of house we were looking at owning. In the end we ended up with a house we wanted, a yard we wanted and at a price that was within our budget.

My purpose in sharing this story is to point out to you what happens when you open yourself up to opportunities. By exploring possibilities, by having conversations with people, you will discover opportunities that you may have never considered. When you know where you want to go, and you are open to any path that will lead you there, roads will open that can take you further and faster than you thought possible.

Ask yourself, how many times have you had a conversation with someone, where in hindsight you realized that you had an opportunity to further your goals?

Creating luck, and increasing the opportunity for luck, to happen is about having clarity on your vision for the future and being open minded about how that future comes to fruition. Do not be like the man who is drowning, waiting for God to come down from the heavens and save him. Take the gifts that life gives you, and build on them, one brick at a time.

Chapter 3

MAKING DREAMS A REALITY

W E ALL WANT TO live a life that is different than the one we have now. We dream of living in a bigger house, traveling more often or spending more time with our families. But how do you turn your dreams into reality?

In this chapter, I am going to talk about the financial side of making our dreams a reality. We are going to discuss how to finance your dreams by tapping into the resources you already have, and we are going to dispel a major myth and misconception in finance, which holds many people back from achieving their dreams.

How Much Will Your Dreams Cost?

The true cost of owning anything is a lot more than just the sticker price. Conventional wisdom offers many suggestions for how to determine cost. You can look at your purchase price, cost of ownership, upfront costs vs ongoing costs. The list is endless, and every advisor will have their own opinion, each of which is perfectly valid.

In this section, we are going to cover some of the basics, at the end I am going to share my personal method for calculating costs, which bucks convention quite a bit.

Regardless of the cost method you use, there are some basic questions you will want to answer:

1. What are the upfront costs?
2. Are there additional one-time costs?
3. Are there recurring costs?
4. How long will it last and what will it cost to replace it?
5. Can you sell it and what will it cost to sell it?

Upfront Costs: These are costs that you will incur on day one. For example, if you buy a car, you have the cost of the car or your initial lease payment. When buying a home, you have Title costs, attorney fees, realtor fees, insurance, loan fees, etc.

Additional Costs: Are there additional fees or one-time expenses that will be related to the purchase? Buying a house, you might have some closing costs or other fees associated with the purchase of your home like inspection and appraisal which would be one-time upfront payments or expenses related to buying it such as title search.

Recurring Costs: This is where most people get tripped up, oftentimes we know what something will cost, but we do not know how much it will cost to maintain.

Continuing with our example of a house. As the house ages it will need various repairs to maintain it, you will have property taxes, utilities, insurance, unexpected repairs etc. These expenses need to be taken into account when estimating the total ownership cost over time. You then need to adjust these costs for inflation.

In a healthy economy, the cost for goods and services will steadily increase overtime. Historically inflation has been at around 3%/year. In 20 years, a $1,000 monthly expense today, will cost you $1806.11. Accounting for the increase in our ongoing costs is critical.

How to Finance Your Dreams?

The good news is that today, more than ever, there are many ways to finance our dreams. It is easy to fall prey to the trap that you need all the money up front. The truth is you don't. In financial planning, there is a tool called "Net Present Value" or NVP.

In layman's terms, NVP is a way to determine how much money you need today in order to have a set sum of money in the future. For instance, say we wanted to buy a $50k boat in 10 years. Assuming we could grow our money at a steady 5%/year, we would need $30,695.66 today in order for us to have the 50k in 10 years.

Using this formula, we could factor in monthly or yearly contributions, and we could flip the formula to help us determine what our ongoing costs are as well.

Of course, we don't really need 50k or even 30k in order to buy our boat today. Thanks to the wonderful world of lending, we can borrow money against our new boat, and finance our purchases this way.

Culturally and religiously, we may have been taught to avoid incurring debt, or paying interest. As with many things in life, similar to fat, cholesterol, or really everything in life. there is good debt and there is bad debt. Since the 2007/8 housing bubble and the great recession there has been a movement to consider all debt as bad.

Yes, debt can be a bad thing - if you are in over your head with credit card bills and student loans. It is easy to feel like the weight of your debt is suffocating or crushing down on you - but that doesn't mean one should avoid all forms of debt.

There are many forms of both good and bad debt. For example, student loans which can provide a degree can improve your earning potential. Contrast this with payday loans, which are designed to trap people into an endless cycle of debt - and should be outlawed.

Bad Debt

Let us take a moment and acknowledge the fear that we have of Bad Debt.

In 2007, most Americans had Adjustable-Rate Mortgages or ARMs. At the time these loans had been given, interest rates were incredibly low, and the market was doing well.

Additionally, because of certain economic pressures at the time, banks had massive incentives to loan people as much money as possible. This led to a rapid increase in housing prices, which led to greater loans, and the cycle repeated itself, until eventually the bubble burst. The average American lost 40% of their net worth virtually overnight, many people found themselves homeless, jobless, and/or with destroyed finances.

What made this debt "bad", was the fact that it was a type of debt that had no fixed rate. The interest rates would change periodically, and it became difficult to know how much you were spending in total on your monthly payments - because the payment amount could change every month! Over a short period of time, people found their, once attractive, low interest rate ARMs, transformed into what we now call "high-interest loans." For many people this caused their monthly payments to jump, from barely affordable to unmanageable.

There is good reason to fear debt, nobody wants to end up homeless, nor do they want to watch as their possessions are sold at auction to pay off their debts. Bad Debt is a debt that is unpredictable, un-affordable, or specifically designed to increase your debt.

Credit Cards and Payday Loans are examples of bad debt, most unsecured loans are perfect examples of bad debt. Unsecured loans is usually typified by adjustable interest rates, so your payment can go up or down, and be unpredictable. Your interest is calculated each month and added to your total, and typically the interest is at a significant rate.

Good Debt

Let us contrast bad debt with good debt. We have all bought or leased cars. Regardless of where interest rates are, car dealerships always seem to have the best loan terms. Why? Because the only way that most people can afford to buy their product is by taking out a loan. Additionally, the loan is secured by the car itself, so the lender's downside is theoretically limited. Car loans and leases are great forms of debt, they are essentially free money. You might be paying more for the car over the life of the loan, but you can almost surely make more money in the markets, or even a Bank CD, than you would save in interest by buying the car outright.

What makes a debt "good":

· Monthly payment amounts are usually fixed and predictable.

· Interest rates are low and competitive.

· The debt is designed to be paid off rather than accumulate more debt.

· Your downside is limited

· It utilizes the equity in your property

In business and investing we call this type of debt "leverage." Leverage is how hedge funds and large corporations increase their returns, by borrowing money to buy more assets. When used responsibly; good debt can be extremely valuable.

Another form of Good Debt is Mortgages and Student Loans. Mortgages allow us to purchase homes, build equity and accumulate value. Student Loans allow us to invest in ourselves and increase the return on our labor. Both forms of loans can be done in ways that are "good" as well as "bad." The key to good debt is to ensure that it meets the characteristics of good debt, and that your downside is limited or protected. The answer to how to protect your downside lay in the exercises you did in the first chapter.

Tapping Your Hidden Assets

There was once a merchant, who lived in a great big mansion, his walls were covered in gold, and he surrounded himself with the trappings of wealth. As our merchant grew older, he found it harder to work and began relying on his accumulated wealth to support himself. One day, when our merchant was old and frail, his money ran out and he found his cupboard's bare of food. Eventually the townspeople found him dead in his kitchen, he had died of starvation surrounded by his gold.

Many of us have wealth, it could be our good credit, or the home equity in our homes, or cars. At some point you need to ask yourself, what is the point of all this accumulated wealth if you don't use it? If you plan on living in your home for the rest of your life, and you need funds for retirement, why not get a reverse mortgage or a traditional mortgage, or a home equity line of credit? Or downsize and cash out on some of that equity.

After my dad died, we discovered that he had racked up thousands of dollars in credit card bills. Literally the last two years of his life, he accumulated massive amounts of unsecured debt. He used it to buy himself guitars and music equipment, things that brought him happiness in those final years. At the end of the day, since the debt was unsecured, the loans were forgiven or written off. My purpose in sharing this story with you is this "use your credit to your advantage."

To be clear, I am not advocating racking up debt that you have no intention of repaying, but what is the harm in having a mortgage that you know you can pay? So, you die with a mortgage? As long as your spouse and loved ones have the resources to continue making payments (which you can ensure through life insurance or your freedom fund.) What skin is it off your back to have a mortgage?

As long as you have a sound financial plan in place, and you have properly weighed the pros and cons, I think you would be remiss in not exploring debt financing as an option with your financial advisor.

Bottom Line: don't leave your hard-earned equity on the table just because it is "unconventional." As always, do some soul searching and ensure that you can live with your decisions, and ensure that your decisions are sound financially and emotionally.

Accelerating Your Dreams

So far in this chapter we have talked about how to quantify your dreams, ways to determine how much money you need, and how to leverage the assets at your disposal.

In this section we are going to bring all these ideas together and discover how you can use these concepts to realize your dreams sooner than you thought possible.

I want to share with you an exercise that I was shown early in my career. I was on a webinar with Frank Kern, who was one of the great marketers at the time. This was early in his career, and as part of his training, he did this little exercise. He wrote on the following on the screen:

Dreams:
- $1 Million Dollar House
- $20k vacation twice a year
- Etc.

Frank went on to explain that you don't actually need a million dollars to live in a million-dollar home, all you need is a mortgage for a million dollars. And so, he wrote the following:

Cost:
- $5000/month Mortgage
- $3500/month vacation savings

Take a moment and let that sink in. Due to how debt works in our country, there is a huge incentive for banks to lend money. The availability of money is regulated by the central banks, and they try to regulate the flow of money in such a way that the economy grows at a steady and sustainable rate.

In a modern economy, you don't need the "full cost" - what you need is the debt maintenance cost. In the old days, banks used to take on the full risk for any loan, so banks were pretty stingy about the types of loans they made. Then debt securitization came about, now banks sell off their loans as derivatives to speculators and investors.

This cycle did get out of control in the mid-2000s and it is what led to the housing bubble, and the great recession of '07/08. However, the debt system was not dismantled. If it is ever disbanded, our debt financing system will have to be replaced with something similar. We live in a consumer economy; we need people to spend money in order for our economy to grow.

Recently with the COVID relief packages, the Federal Government has doubled down on this view, and economists are being forced to recognize the merits of this type of debt financing.

To be clear, all parties involved want to loan you the money to be able to finance your home, your boat, your car, etc.... and they are willing to let you use their money in exchange for the interest you will pay them. There are also lots of really good financial reasons why you should finance your home, car or boat even if you could own it outright, and we will explore those reasons in later chapters.

Bottom Line: To achieve your dreams you need to be able to define them and quantify them financially. Once you have a number, you can possibly use good debt and your hidden assets to finance your dreams, possibly accelerating the realization of your dreams. As always, this should be done responsibly and in the context of your overall financial plan, which we will get to in the next chapters.

Chapter 4

THE 5-MINUTE PLAN

I N THE LAST TWO chapters, we discussed how to define your goals physically, emotionally and financially. In this chapter, we arc going to talk about how we turn those goals into reality. Specifically, how to create a plan and decision-making process that takes you from point A to point B, and helps you navigate the bumps along the road.

One of the reasons, why financial plans fail is because they are massive documents and are generally not available when making decisions. Life is the sum of thousands of individual decisions, each decision compounding to bring us the whole. Getting your Starbucks Latte, or ordering in for dinner, these may not seem like decisions that can affect the outcome of our lives. However, thousands, or tens of thousands of these tiny decisions, made over the course of a lifetime, will change the path of our destiny.

In order for a financial plan to succeed, it needs to be a habit, it needs to be something you can easily do. and practice each time you have a financial decision.

You need a framework for ensuring that you are always making the best decision for yourself and your loved ones; regardless of whether that decision is to eat out, buy a new car or take a vacation.

In this chapter, we are going to walk through *The 5-minute Plan,* it is a decision making framework that you can use for making every financial decision.

The Plan

The 5-Minute Plan is a way of evaluating decisions from a financial perspective. It is a method for determining if decisions are aligned with your goals and objectives, and for determining what the best decision is for yourself and our loved ones.

When you have a process in place, a process that is based on facts and logic, and one that accounts for your emotional and financial needs, you are able to feel confident in your choices, and you are able to sleep better at night knowing that you are making the best decision - given your current life goals and priorities in life.

Life choices are rarely black and white, they are usually shades of grey. Your decision-making process needs to account for this reality of life. Personally, when I evaluate decisions, I use a two-step process. The first step of the process is to quantify the decision. Understanding the choice, you are making is important, and the bigger the decision. the more time I spend evaluating.

When making financial decisions, there are several basic questions you always need to ask:

1. Does this bring me closer to my goals?
2. What is my downside if I say yes?
3. What is my downside if I say No?
4. What are my potential upsides?
5. What is the probability of success?
6. Does this decision need to be made now?
7. Is the risk/reward worthwhile?
8. Does this endanger my Financial Freedom?

The first few times you go through this process, it will take you some time. The more you go through the process, the easier and faster it will get, until it becomes second nature.

The real magic in this process comes from the first question: does this bring me closer to my goals? This is a question that will change over time, and as you develop your decision-making skills, you will probably add complexity to your goals, and possibly use both positive and negative goals.

In the beginning, I recommend starting with a simple and easy to articulate goal.

Returning to our list of questions, once you have the answers to these questions, the decision you are currently should be fairly obvious. Either the choice will bring you closer to your goals, without undermining your financial freedom - or it will hurt your goals. In which case you need to make the determination: if the short-term benefits outweigh your long-term goals.

No judgment either way, just be honest with yourself when you make the choice. As a serial entrepreneur, I habitually sacrifice short-term benefits for mid- to long-term goals. I also take risk/reward choices that would make my wife cringe... part of the reason why we still have separate finances.

Q1: Does this bring me closer to my goals?

The key to success is prioritization. As Steven Covey says, "Priorities Determine Your Destiny." If we focus on our most important goals, the goal that will make the biggest impact on our life and our happiness, and we are crystal clear about our priorities, then we will find our decision-making process becomes easier.

Ask yourself, what is your most important goal today? What is the goal that you are willing to stay up late, get up early, and go that extra mile to accomplish? Whatever that goal is, that is the lens through which you should evaluate all your decisions. You can and should have secondary goals, but they are goals of opportunity, and they should not detract from your primary goal.

Q2: What is my downside if I say yes?

This is a trick question. Take your time to really think through the answer. Look beyond the obvious downside of "being out the cash." The choices we make in life have repercussions, they have impacts on the range of our future choices. Using the example of buying a home, when you purchase a home or choose a place to live, it will anchor you or your wealth to a specific location for a period of time. This will have a downstream impact on the choices available to you.

Q3: What is my downside if I say No?

In addition to the obvious financial downsides, what are the emotional ones? Will you regret this decision in 10, 20, or 50 years? In my humble opinion, living a life without regrets is one of the secrets to happiness. It is hard when you are married, have business partners, and obligations, however the more regrets you have the more unhappy you will become.

Q4: What is my potential upside?

Notice that I use the word potential. Nothing in life is guaranteed, you can have the most iron clad contract, you could be holding the pot of gold in your hand, and it still might not be guaranteed. The company could go bust, laws could change, what your holding might be a fake, or it could be seized from you tomorrow. We have all experienced this in one form or another, whether it was a parent taking away a favorite toy or missing out on a deal. If the upside was guaranteed, there would be a lot more wealthier people walking around than there are today. So, ask yourself, if everything goes the way you think, what is your potential upside?

Q5: What is your probability of success?

Realistically, based on your accumulated life experiences; based on your experiences watching other people fail repeatedly. What do you think is the realistic chance of this decision turning out well? 50%, 75%, 100%? Maybe it will turn out okay, but what is the chance you will realize your decisions full upside potential? The more realistic you can be in your answer the better off you will be. Life rarely turns out the way we expect. There are always hidden costs, speed bumps, and potholes along the way. Success never looks like how we imagined. Be realistic in your estimation of how likely this venture will succeed.

Q6: Does this decision need to be made now?

Of all the questions we ask, this is probably the hardest one to answer. Scarcity is an emotional hot button, it taps directly into our lizard brain and fires all kinds of signals. Scarcity tells us we have to do this action now or we will go hungry! It screams and yells at us to take action! T

he world of marketing and sales knows this about our lizard brain, and they work scarcity and hot buttons into everything they do. Everything is scarce, there is always a reason why you have to act now or you will miss out!

Personally, as soon as I hear a salesperson start down the scarcity path, I walk away. There are times when scarcity is real, but it will never be as scarce as portrayed. Overcoming or redirecting this basic human urge, is a skill you need to develop, if you want to be financially successful. Few things in life are life and death, keep this fact in perspective as you make decisions.

An interesting tidbit that helps me: veterans generally make good business leaders. Partially this is due to the skills they learn in the military, and partially because they were in life and death situations on a regular basis. Vets have faced real threats to their life, as such they recognize the false colors of anxiety masquerading as a life and death threats.

Personally, whenever I feel my lizard brain trying to convince me that I MUST make this decision. I just remind myself that nobody is trying to kill me, and I will be perfectly fine regardless of the decision I make today. This exercise helps quite the insane urgency of the lizard brain and over-time teaches it to recognize what is actually important vs what society tells us is important.

Q7: Is the risk/reward worthwhile?

After answering the previous questions, you should have a good idea about the answer to the question "is the risk/reward worthwhile?"

It goes without saying, you will never be perfect at answering this question. The truth is that anyone who claims to have the secret sauce for answering this question, is either a moron or a charlatan, either way they will lose their money shortly.

Life will always surprise you with new twists and turns, just as you think you know the rules, they will change on you. The key is to constantly be working to improve your understanding and knowledge and take your time to evaluate your decisions as best as possible. Asking yourself these questions, honestly, and without judgment, will put you head and shoulders above your peers.

Q8: Does this endanger my Financial Freedom?

In the first chapter, we worked hard to define what financial freedom means to you, and what it would take for you to achieve financial freedom. As we go through life, we need to protect our hard-earned freedom. Ideally, we don't want to risk our freedom, or when we do risk it, we want to ensure it is for the right reasons – which are wrothwhile and have a high probability of success.

***

In reviewing and answering the 5-minute plan questions, most decisions will become obvious. You will also learn where your knowledge gaps lay, and what are the types of decisions you are ill equipped to answer. As the old saying goes, experience is the thing that you get after you need it. The goal of asking these questions is to identify decisions that don't have favorable outcomes and identify where our knowledge and experience gaps lay.

In the later chapters of this book, we are going to go over some of the basics financial knowledge that you MUST know if you are going to make sound financial decisions. Oftentimes the facts you don't know are what hurt you the most.

As you evaluate decisions, if you feel unsure or uncertain about your answers, discuss them with your significant other, discuss them with your friends, and find professionals who are subject matter experts who can provide you with their insight and advice.

At all times, if your advisors cannot explain their answers, or their answers don't make sense to you - do not accept them, they are probably wrong.

Finance is simple, it is people who make it complicated. **Remember, if it is not simple then it is wrong!** Keep searching for the simple answer that explains your known facts, when you have that answer you will have the truth or be significantly close to the truth.

Chapter 5

PROTECTING YOUR DOWNSIDE

WE LIVE IN A world constantly bombarded with information. The more choices we have, the harder it is to make decisions. One of the most important concepts in finance is protecting your losses or downside risk.

Protecting your downside, means taking precautions to avoid failure. Protecting your downside will generally ensures long term success, in finance, and in all areas of life. There are times when you need to put it all on the line and take significant risks. However, when you follow *The 5-Minute Plan* process, when you have protected your emotional, financial, and physical downsides, when you ask the right questions, and only make educated decisions – then you have already limited your downside significantly, or at least quantified and mentally prepared for its potential outcome.

In this chapter, we are going to discuss some of the common and uncommon downside risks, and methods for hedging or protecting against unwanted outcomes.

Types of Downside Risk

There are several types of downside risks that we need to be concerned about. Once we understand the types of risks we face, we can then explore methods of protection.

High Frequency and Low Impact Risks:

These are risks that we usually take for granted, such as catching the flu or the common cold. Another perfect example is a toilet clogging. You know at some point your toiled is going to get clogged. You also know that the cost to get it fixed can be as simple as plunging your toilet, or as costly as hiring a plumber for a few hundred dollars. Most of us are willing to accept this type of risk and pay for the expense when it occurs, either in the form of buying a plunger ($10) and spending our time, or in hiring a plumber.

As we get older, or as our time becomes more valuable, we many no longer wish to assume these risks. We might offload these risks by living in a condo or community where those services are provided by the building or community.

Medical expenses are a great example of how this type of risk changes over time. When we are younger and healthier, our medical expenses are generally lower. As we get older, our medical expenses become more frequent and grow in cost. At some point the cumulative cost, even for the "low impact" event of seeing the doctor, or of paying for routine medicines, will become excessive. At some point it will become important to have good medical insurance to cover these low impact, high frequency costs.

When evaluating financial decisions, we need to look at the cost for the "high probability, low impact" events that are associated with our decision and either account for the ongoing cost, or the cost for insurance to mitigate our downside. We will discuss the role of insurance in later chapters.

Low Frequency and High Impact Risks:

On the flip side, there are some risks that do not occur frequently, but when they do occur, they can be expensive. Think of a car accident, fire in your home, lawsuit, hospitalization etc. These are examples of events, they don't occur frequently, and when they do occur, they can be devastating. These are the types of events you want to insurance and protect against.

Insurance is a means of transferring risk. For example, when you insure your house, the insurance company takes on some of the financial risks associated with homeownership, such as paying for any expenses if something happens to it (like fire or theft). In return, you pay a premium and accept certain limitations on coverage.

You can dial the risks covered and associated limitations of your policy to fit your budget and emotional and financial comfort levels. We will talk more about this in later chapters. For now, the important concept to know is that almost any risk can be transferred to an insurance company, for a fee.

Systemic Risks:

Warning: we are going to start diving into some weeds here. Up until now we have been talking about risks that are general in nature, and that are probably familiar. Understanding the next set of concepts is critical to your long-term financial success, the greater your mastery of these concepts the more wealth you will accumulate.

Systemic risk is the risk that affects not just an individual person or institution but the entire system.

Starting small, one way to think about "systemic risk" is to think about a natural disaster. When a natural disaster hits, it does not just affect one house, it affects an entire city. You may be thinking to yourself: Great! if it affects everyone then I will recover the same way that everyone else recovers. This is a mistake; this is a fallacy that most people make. What you don't see is the cost that most people incurred to recover. You don't see how it affected their life savings, how it set them back from retirement, or the stresses they experienced.

There are not many ways to protect yourself from systemic risks. They do exist, they usually take a bit of research and due diligence to discover, and they usually mean a tradeoff of some sort to protect against.

Because systemic risks affect large populations, the typical methods for transferring risk i.e. via insurance, is usually not available. Systemic risk is the one of the few things that can instantly put an insurance company out of business. In some cases of systemic risk or disasters, the Government will provide insurance, such as Flood or Tornado Insurance, in other cases they provide funding in the form of loans, grants, stimulus checks, cutting interest rates, welfare programs, tax changes, etc. Such as what happened during The Great Recession or COVID-19.

It is important to note, systemic risks can affect the whole economy, and depending on the scale, they can impact the entire world, such as a depression or recession in a global trade partner.

There are also systemic risks associated with the system itself. For instance, blockchain, if someone were to figure out a way to compromise the integrity of the blockchain technology, or a new technology came out that was better, it could wipe out the entire blockchain sector, and all the companies connected to it, overnight. Similarly, if the integrity of the Federal Reserve, or the world's Central Banks were compromised, it is very likely that our entire financial system would experience massive turmoil.

In every decision you make, you will have to take the time to research the systemic risks associated. You will need to discover, what is and is not covered by your insurance companies. You will need to discover how you can protect yourself - and understand what risks that will NOT be covered that you will be forced to assume.

In going through this process, you may discover the need to increase your "financial freedom fund" to cover such eventualities, or perhaps you will create a specific "rainy day" fund, pun intended, for these specific eventualities.

You could also curtail your activities to help mitigate some of those systemic risks, or you could choose to share the risk with others. This evaluation needs to be a continual process, systemic risks are constantly changing, and new threats are emerging. A good financial advisor can advise you on your risks and help you stay current. A good advisor can monitor these risks for you so, they don't derail your goals and lifestyle.

Non-Systemic, Political and Legal Risks:

Non-systemic risks are specific to a particular situation. A good example would be buying a house that was built in the 1950s. The house will probably have an old AC, the pipes might be corroding, laws may have changed, taxes may go up or down. Phrased another way, non-systemic risk is the risk that the status quo will change.

Ask yourself, if the status quo changed, would I still want to make this choice? What is the probability of the status quo changing, in the near-, mid-, or long-term future? Will those probabilities change my decision?

One example, my mother-in-law lives in a Condo in Florida, to her the pool and services provided by the building are the reasons she chose to live there. If the building no longer had a pool, or no longer provided the services she needs, she would find another place to live.

To help get your mind thinking of the possibilities, another example is me and my wife, we love the community we live in. Its proximity to my wife's job, the schools and the people. My wife recently got a new job, and the demographics of our community have changed. The underlying reasons for living here have changed, and we must re-evaluate if this is the place where we want to live. If we choose to move we will incur costs, and depending on the market, and the urgency of the move, it may mean losing money on our custom-built home. Being conscience of this possibility, when we built our home, we didn't buy top of the line appliances, and we didn't spend money, as if this was our forever home. This is a perfect example of using The 5-minute plan process to make sound financial decisions.

The Inevitable:

To quote Benjamin Franklin "in this world, nothing is certain except death and taxes." There is an inevitability in all decisions. Cars will need repair, and eventually they will stop working. Homes require maintenance, people require medicine, and all good things must come to an end.

In evaluating our decisions, we must keep this reality in mind. All things deteriorate, and maintenance, repairs, healing, become more expensive with age, eventually we will not be able to maintain "it" - and eventually life will come to an end. Planning for those eventualities is a must. The more we plan upfront, the less of a burden it will be, on our finances and loved ones, when the time comes.

A Note About Investments:

As I am sure you have heard, the key to successful investing is to "Buy low and sell high." A task that is easier said than done. Protecting your investments from market risks, follow the same rules as any other risks. The specifics of how to go about enacting that protection are diverse and many. I will provide some specifics later in this book, and I will write more in my upcoming book on investing.

Key Lessons:

The key lesson in this chapter is to know your risks, do your best to understand your potential downside, ie know what you will lose if it all goes wrong, and make active decisions about the risks you want to assume, and which you will share or transfer to others.

Oftentimes, when examining bad financial choices, you will discover that the choice itself isn't bad - it was the unknown downsides that were the real kicker. The more we can avoid the school of hard knocks, the more we can hedge our downside risk, the better your financial outcomes.

Remember, finance is simple, people make it complicated. Take the time to really explore and understand the risks associated with your decision. Do your own research and make sure that the risk/reward paradigm makes sense to you. If you don't fully understand the risk, know that there are probably hidden dangers, which will come knocking at the most inopportune moments.

Chapter 6

MINIMIZING UNNECESSARY TAXATION

A WHILE BACK, THERE WAS a video that went viral of a father teaching his 3-year-old daughter the meaning of taxes. They are each holding ice cream cones, and the dad says, "before you eat it, I need to take taxes." He then proceeds to take a big bite. "Social Security and Medicare" he takes a smaller bite. The kid is now tearing up. "One more bite, this is a small one, this is city taxes" he says as he takes a final nibble. Now enjoy, proclaims the dad. The kid is mortified.

If you are trying to find a way to save money or reduce losses, then you must consider tax minimization. In fact, dollar for dollar, managing your tax liability might provide a better return on investment than most investment returns.

Think of taxes as building your house on quicksand, each brick you lay slowly sinks into the ground. By the time you are done building, your two-story home is a one-floor walk-in.

Tax minimization is really the epitome of a penny saved is a penny earned. Every dollar you save from unnecessary taxation is another dollar you can put away into your freedom fund, or your retirement savings, which can accumulate into untold wealth over time.

In this chapter, we are going to explore the difference between tax planning and tax preparation. We are going to talk about some of the common minimization techniques you can use, and how to implement them in your life.

Tax Planning vs Tax Preparation

In my experience, there are two primary reasons why people don't take advantage of the tax code to the fullest. The first is they assume it is their patriotic duty to pay the most taxes. It is not. If you google the "taxpayer bill of rights." Right on the IRS's website you will see the following:

⍟IRS

The Right to Pay No More than the Correct Amount of Tax

Taxpayers have the right to pay only the amount of tax legally due, including interest and penalties, and to have the IRS apply all tax payments properly.

There is no reason to pay a penny more than what is legally required. If a credit or exclusion exists, it is your duty to use it.

If you want to provide the government more money to fund programs, buy municipal bonds, your local governments need your money more than the Federal Government. The Federal Government can print more money, local governments cannot.

To be clear, I am not advocating tax evasion, which is illegal. I am advocating taking advantage of the tax code to minimize your tax liability, also known as Tax Avoidance.

The second reason why most people overpay on their taxes, is a misunderstanding of the difference between tax planning and tax preparation.

Tax Preparation is when you give your CPA or Accountant a list of your bills during the year and they prepare your tax return. During this process your tax preparer will see what credits and exclusions you qualify for, and hopefully, if they are good at their jobs, they will help you calculate the correct amount to pay in taxes. If they make a mistake, there is a period where you can go back and refile your returns and correct and under/overpayments.

Tax Planning is proactive, it looks at the tax code, looks at your activities and asks the question "what can you do to reduce your current tax liability." A good accountant or financial advisor will look to the future as well and create a balance between reducing current year tax liability and future tax liability.

By adjusting your actions during the tax year, you can position yourself to take advantage of all the tax opportunities available to you. A common example you are probably familiar with, a contribution to an IRA or 401k. When contributing to retirement accounts, you get a current tax deduction, and you can also potentially earn a tax credit as well, which can further reduce your tax liability.

Exclusions, Deductions, and Credits

There are three basic ways to reduce your tax liability.

Exclusions: Tax exclusions, sometimes referred to as exemptions, is money that don't have to report on your tax return. Examples are certain gifts, profits from selling a home that you have lived in, proceeds from most life insurance policies, etc.. It is called an exclusion, because the amount doesn't even appear on your tax return.

Deductions: Deductions are money that you report on your tax return, however, you don't have to pay taxes on some, or all of these funds. These monies make up your "Adjusted Gross Income" or AGI. Examples of deductions include charitable donations, some interest expenses and home office expenses.

The most common is the "standard deduction", which is a flat dollar amount that congress lets you take, regardless of how much income you have spent/earned in qualifying categories. Depending on your record keeping and your tax preparer, they are probably pretty good at determining which of these numbers will get you the bigger tax benefit.

The key is to balance your deductions related to losses and retirement savings. when managed properly this can lead to significant tax savings. We will discuss specifics later in this chapter.

Credits: Credits are the most valuable of our tax incentives. Credits are amounts of money that the government allows you to take directly from your tax bill.

Say your tax bill was $100 and you qualify for a $10 tax credit, you only need to pay $90 in taxes. Some Credits are "refundable", which means that if you have more credits than you owe in taxes, the IRS will cut you a check for the remainder. This is one of the ways that our government enacts social policy and wealth redistribution.

Most people are familiar with credits, in terms of getting a refund at the end of the year. In reality most people have overpaid their taxes and the IRS is just returning their overpayment. For some people, generally those with lower income, or people who have significant losses, they may qualify for some of the refundable tax credits.

Tax Minimization Strategies

The tax code is constantly changing, every president and every politician has their own idea of how the tax code should be rewritten. As I write this book, we have recently elected a new president, and there are major discussions on increasing taxes. Instead of focusing on tactics that can change with each administration, we are going to focus on strategies that have historically withstood the test of time.

Among the many purposes for taxes, governments use taxes to promote social agendas and economic behaviors. The way taxes are used to promote economic behaviors, is through the use of exclusions, deductions, and credits, colloquially known as "loopholes."

Regardless of the administration, there will always be economic activity that the government wants to incentivize. Generally speaking, the government will encourage activities that grow the economy and reduce future tax burdens. In the US this means that the tax code favors businesses and retirement savings.

Using this knowledge, we can look at the tax code and our activities, and attempt to align the two. The more aligned our actions are with the governments desired actions, the more tax benefits we will generally receive. For example, if you own a business there are more tax options available to you than if you are an employee. Investors who fund businesses over the long haul, receive tax incentives in the form of lower capital gains taxes. Employees who save for their retirement receive incentives, deductions and credits on their tax bill.

Paying a professional to help you identify ways to maximize the tax incentives available to you, by changing your actions, will generally pay off in the long run.

Tax Timing

Another strategy that one could use is tax timing. Timing when you realize income is one of the most powerful tools that businesses and the affluent leverage to their advantage. It is a tool that most taxpayers have available, if they know how to use it. At its core tax timing, it is about deciding when income will show up on your tax return as "taxable" income. It goes without saying that I am not advocating tax evasion, rather legal methods for avoiding the recognition of income.

As a business owner, depending on your accounting method, you may have the ability to prepay expenses, delay invoicing, or engage in other activities that will delay the earnings of income, or accelerate the payment of expenses.

A perfect example would be paying a bill on Dec 31st instead of January 1st, which would affect which tax year the expense would be on. If you are in a year where you made a lot of income, reducing your taxable income may be advantageous, conversely, in a low-income year the opposite would be true.

The same rules apply to individuals. As individuals we may not have as much control of our income, or we may not be able to afford to delay our income. However, knowing that possibility can help us leverage it when the options are available.

Marginal vs Effective Tax Rates:

The reason why tax timing is important is because of the difference between marginal and effective tax rates. In the United States, we use a progress tax system. This means that as you make more money, each "bracket" or group of money is taxed at a different rate.

In the example below, you can see the hypothetical tax for a couple making $110,000. Their Marginal tax rate, or the rate at which their last dollar earned is taxed, is 22%. Conventional wisdom and the media would have you believe that the couple is paying 22% in taxes (which would be about $24k.) However, due to exclusions, and the progressive nature of our tax system, our couple is only paying an effective tax rate of about 10%. if we factored in credits and deductions, they could probably reduce their tax bill even further.

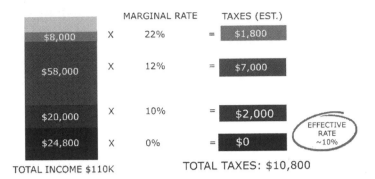

		MARGINAL RATE		TAXES (EST.)
$8,000	X	22%	=	$1,800
$58,000	X	12%	=	$7,000
$20,000	X	10%	=	$2,000
$24,800	X	0%	=	$0

EFFECTIVE RATE ~10%

TOTAL INCOME $110K   TOTAL TAXES: $10,800

Once you start to fully understand our tax system, you can begin doing some real tax planning. For instance, in years where the couple has less income; maybe as they near retirement, or are between jobs, or in years where they have deductible losses, we can take advantage of their lower marginal tax rates. We will discuss some specific strategies later in this chapter. For now, I want you to recognize the difference between marginal and effective tax rates, and the importance of controlling your taxable income.

Some examples of ways that individuals can control their taxable income is through the use of qualified and non-qualified savings accounts.

Qualified Activity & Accounts:

Generally speaking, when we engage in activities that the tax code incentivizes, it is considered a "qualified" activity. The biggest example is retirement accounts. In the US, at the time I am writing this book, and for the last 40 years or so, congress has incentivized various types of savings.

To help encourage people to save, they have created special tax incentives that say: if you put money away in these accounts, and you only use them for the uses we outline, either the principal that you contribute to the account, and/or the growth will be tax free. The tax-free status, may be at the time of contribution or at the time of distribution, depending on the type of account.

I know this is a little vague, bear with me as I explain the principals and then we will dive into the details. It is critically important to understand the principals, because the details can and do change from one administration to the next, however Politicians aren't the most creative people, so the principles are unlikely to change much over time.

The Tax Efficiency Ladder

There is an unspoken golden rule about taxes, the government will always get their pound of flesh. There is no way to really avoid paying taxes; you can choose when you pay taxes, and you may be able to control how much you pay in taxes - but you will almost never avoid actually paying taxes. Keeping this golden rule in mind, I want to introduce you to a little concept I like to call the *Tax Efficiency Ladder.*

Highest Level
Tax Me When I Choose Accounts

Middle Level
Tax Me Later Accounts

Lowest Level
Tax Me Now Accounts

At the bottom rung of our ladder, we have the "Tax Me Now Accounts", these are your checking, savings, brokerage accounts, etc. These are the accounts where you pay taxes as you earn money.

Tax Me Later Accounts:

Tax me later accounts are a subset of the qualified accounts that we discussed earlier. The qualified accounts can be broken down into two categories, the "pre-taxed" and the "tax me later."

In the "Tax Me Later" group, we have our standard retirement accounts, like our 401k, 403(b), Individual Retirement Accounts (IRA), etc. Contributions to these accounts are not taxed, and they grow tax free, however, when it comes time to withdraw our money, the IRS is going to tax it as "ordinary income."

To help ensure that the government gets their pound of flesh, they mandate "Required Minimum Distributions" or RMDs. These distributions are specifically designed to drain your entire "qualified" savings during your lifetime and accelerate the distributions in the early years of your retirement, when you most likely need it the least.

This will have the effect of converting your "qualified" assets into assets that will be subject to regular and ongoing taxation. (And if you have the gall to die early, they require that your non-spouse heirs drain your accounts within 10-years...)

The money in the "tax me later" tier is great, it helps us build savings, however it is a future tax liability that we do not control. As we go through life, we always want to look for opportunities to convert some of our "tax me later" money into "tax me when I choose" money.

Tax Me When I Choose:

These are what most would consider to be the most tax efficient of our "qualified" accounts. These are similar to the "tax me later" accounts, except we have already paid taxes on these accounts. This allows us to grow our assets tax free and at the time I am writing this book, RMDs are not required, and the growth is tax free, as long as it is a "qualified" distribution.

As discussed earlier, controlling your taxable income is advantageous because it allows you to control when, and at what marginal and effective tax rate, you pay taxes. In years where we have significant taxable earnings, and our marginal tax rate is high, we can reduce our tax liability by contributing to our "tax me later" accounts. In years where our taxable income is lower, we can load up our tax brackets and convert our "tax me later" money into "tax me when I choose," which can be "tax-free" upon distribution.

There is another benefit to this conversion. The money that is in the "tax me later" accounts, continue to grow tax-free until they are withdrawn at a date and time of your choosing (unless we die.) Contrast that with the "tax me later" accounts where the tax benefits on the growth terminate upon withdrawal - which is predetermined by congress.

***

The more you can use the tax code to your advantage, the more wealth you will be able to accumulate. Congress is counting on the millions of Americans who don't take the time to work on the system; they are counting on you to do the bare minimum to save on your taxes.

All you need is a little bit of know-how and foresight to take control of your taxes. Next time you speak to your accountant or financial advisor, ask them how they can help you reduce your taxes this year and in the future. Make sure you speak with your advisors, share with them your current short- and long-term goals so they can help you account for them in your tax planning. Many financial advisors and accountants have sophisticated software that can help you identify hidden opportunities; you just need to know how to ask.

As always, this book is designed to be general in nature, while I have done my best to ensure that the information is accurate, the tax code and strategies are constantly changing and may be different for you where you live. Consult with a licensed tax professional before taking any action.

Chapter 7

PLANNING FOR THE UNEXPECTED

LIFE IS FULL OF unexpected surprises, which is why it is so important to be prepared for every outcome, or at the very least prepared for some of the more devastating outcomes.

Over the course of my career, I have personally worked with hundreds of Financial Advisors. One theme that is common among the best advisors is that they all had a personal story of how themselves or their family were devastated by a lack of planning.

I remember one advisor, who told me how he went from running an aircraft maintenance company to being one of the top advisors in his city. He became an advisor after watching his mother hand over her wedding ring in bankruptcy court - all because his dad had died and had not taken the time to ensure that his company had a succession plan. As is the case in most states, when a company is owned by a single individual, typically the state will close the company upon death of the owner – unless the articles of incorporation allow for the assignment of shares upon death. In our advisors' case, the state closed the company and creditors liquidated every asset in his name to pay for his outstanding debts.

Personally, when I was 19, my home was gutted in a fire. Nobody was hurt, but all our possessions were destroyed. My dad had an amazing homeowners insurance policy at the time, and he ended up maxing out the policy, which gave me the seed money to start my business. My story could have easily turned out very differently, if my dad had a cheaper policy, one that didn't cover relocation expenses, or one that covered the value of the home instead of the replacement cost.

In this chapter we are going to dive into specifics on some of the most common risks and how to hedge and mitigate their financial impact.

Property

We are all familiar with renters and homeowners insurance. At its core it will help make us whole if there is unexpected damage to our home, or if someone gets hurt on our property. These are low frequency events, however when they do occur, they can be extremely expensive. There are some key factors you may want to ensure your policy covers:

Replacement Cost:

The difference between replacement costs and value insurance. A replacement policy covers the full expense of replacing any property that is lost or damaged.

A value insurance policy will only pay for an item's depreciated value, which usually isn't as much as it would cost to replace. A good example would be a car, the second you drive a car off the dealership lot the value of the car depreciates. The value policy will pay the depreciated value and a replacement policy will reimburse you for the cost of replacing your vehicle with the same or similar. If you lease a car, most companies will require that you have this type of insurance or have something called gap insurance, which covers the difference between what the insurance company pays and the contractual value of the car.

Imagine for a second that something happens to your home, and your property needs to be replaced. The "value" of your used couch is not the cost to replace it. The few bucks you save by having a cheaper policy is not worth the expense of having to shell out more cash in the event of a claim.

Limits and Property Value:

You want to check these numbers often; many times, people will buy a policy and they will continually renew it without updating the limits. Due to inflation, the cost to repair or replace your home and belongings will continually increase. Take the time to ensure that the limits are still in line with the cost, if they aren't asking them to increase the limits. Also ensure that you understand the exclusions, many policies will have exclusions for things like jewelry that is over a specified dollar amount, unless they are specifically named in the policy.

If your policy limits are substantially less than your net worth, purchase an umbrella policy. An umbrella policy is a good way to protect yourself against large claims. This kind of insurance covers you in case you're liable for damages over and above your car or homeowners insurance limits. Think of it as a supplemental insurance policy. It is generally pretty cost effective, and a must if you have significant assets.

Guest Coverage:

It is important to ensure that your policy has adequate coverage for guests. Growing up, one of my friends, his grandmother tripped and fell in their apartment, she did not have any health insurance and their policy maxed out at $5,000 for guest health benefits. If she wasn't family, she could have sued them for thousands of dollars for her treatment.

Health

Due to the way health insurance is currently structured in the United States, my only recommendation is to contact a good health insurance broker (not an agent) and have them walk you through all your options. As a business owner there are a lot more options available than to individuals. As with all types of insurance, you want to make sure you understand what it covers and what it doesn't cover and make the decision that is best for your financial and emotional wellbeing. In addition to your standard health insurance, there are specialty policies like cancer insurance, long term care insurance, and others that are limited in their coverage, but offer benefits that may not be included in your current health insurance.

Disability

Disability insurance is a policy that can be purchased to protect your income, if a person becomes unable to work due to an injury or covered illness. There are two basic types of disability insurance: short term and long-term disability insurance.

The short term is designed to cover the period before you qualify for long term benefits, or to cover things like pregnancy or minor injuries. Workers' compensation and paid maternity leave may provide similar coverage in your state.

Long-term disability coverage comes in two flavors: those that are designed to cover you until you qualify for Social Security Disability and those that are designed to replace incomes for high-earning individuals whose income will not be adequately replaced by Social Security. If you are a highly specialized practitioner or high-income earner with nontransferable skills, like a surgeon, then you absolutely must have long term disability insurance, especially if you want insurance that will cover you if you can't work in your profession.

There is a cheaper form of disability insurance that only covers you if you cannot find *any* work, which is a very broad category and can be quite difficult to qualify for long term benefits.

Home/Car Warranties

A home warranty policy is a contract that you can purchase to protect yourself against expensive repairs and maintenance on your house. If something breaks in your home, the company will either repair it, or replace it for you. home warranties are a great way to protect your home. They can cover things like plumbing and electrical appliances. Typically home warranties cover items not covered by traditional your home or renters insurance policies.

Home/Car Warranties are sold as insurance, but they are not run, nor are they managed by regulated insurance companies. In reality, these home warranty companies contract with service providers for flat fee services, typically this will be your "co-pay" amount. In exchange for providing services at a flat rate, the service provider gets a steady stream of low-paying gigs when business is slow.

In theory, home warranties should be a win-win proposition. However, due to human nature, the people who are the most expensive to insure are the ones that seek coverage the most. This applies equally to customers as well as vendors, creating sub-optimal conditions for both. In regulated insurance, the government oversees the insurance company and their client base to ensure that the companies are profitable and providing adequate service. As a result, you need to buy these policies with your eyes open.

Who is a home warranty policy right for? If you have an old home that has aging appliances or will need repairs in the near future - and you have the time to call and supervise the vendors and ensure that they return with the parts, and they don't try to continually charge you new service fees, then you will probably benefit from a home warranty.

The best way to demonstrate the pros and cons is with a real-life example.

The first house that my wife and I lived in was built in the 50s, the appliances were from the 80s, and in the community, we were living in the water was corroding the old copper pipes, leaks were common. We got a home warranty, within a year we had our washer and dryer replaced, and the plumbing in our home was replaced. We were without a washer and dryer for several weeks while we waited for "parts" and "scheduling" and they did repair it once, and it broke again a few months later. All of that was inconvenient, however, I worked from home and my work wasn't busy at the time, so I had the time. Our home warranty that we paid maybe $1,000 for benefited us about $2,000, possibly more. Of course, we cancelled the policy immediately afterward the dryer and washer were replaced, at that point the total replacement cost for items covered by the warranty and the probability of them failing were low enough that it was questionable if we would break even. As it was, we didn't need another repair/replacement for 4-5 years. During this time the home warranty company would have recouped their money and then some.

The second story is about my mother. She had a home warranty, but she did not have the time to be on top of the repair people. Her central AC stopped working, the workers came out and repaired it. It stopped working a week later. Her repair technicians managed to charge her for six visits before they eventually replaced the unit. Meanwhile, she was without AC for the entire summer.

Are home warranties worthwhile? It really depends on your home and your ability to manage the repair service.

Supplemental/Incident Based Insurance

A number of insurance providers provide cash benefits when certain events occur. The policies can be used to pay for medical or related expenses, or they can act as compensation for a loss - such as an Accidental Death & Dismemberment Policy. These policies are generally cheaper than traditional insurance - because their benefits amounts and conditions for payment are severely limited.

These types of policies can be used to help pay costs during short term disabilities and injuries or pay for specific expenses like long term facilities that may not be covered by your specific insurance. When thinking about your freedom fund, when you are still growing your fund, supplemental insurance is a great source of emergency funding.

Business, Umbrella, and Specialty Insurance

If you are a business owner, professional, or someone whose work can cost another individual significant amount of money, or their life (like a healthcare worker) then you want to ensure that you have professional liability insurance.

Generally speaking, personal insurance policies will specifically exclude business activities, this may even include your home office. Businesses can purchase their own insurance that protects their business, its property, employees and directors.

If you are an employee, you should also carry professional liability insurance; a company's policy will protect the company - potentially at your expense. As mentioned earlier, an umbrella policy covers you in case you are liable for damages not covered by your other policies. This is a must if you have significant assets.

You should also be aware that any activity that carries a high financial risk - probably has a specific designed insurance policy that you can purchase. For example, as a financial advisor, I can purchase "transfer insurance" which means that if someone fraudulently has funds transferred from a client account, the insurance policy may protect my firm and my clients, up to specified dollar amounts, subject to the restrictions of the policy. Cyber security is another example of a specific type of insurance policy that covers a very narrow set of circumstances. If there is an activity that could potentially cost you significant time, money, or threaten your financial well-being then it is worth discussing with your insurance brokers/advisors. Taking the time to discover the types of coverage available to you will pay dividends in the long run.

***

Riders and Ancillary Benefits:

Ask about ancillary benefits that may be beneficial to you. For example, many auto insurers have roadside assistance or loaner vehicle riders that can be added for a few dollars each month. If you have a second home or a rental property, adding it as a rider to your homeowners policy may be cheaper than purchasing a separate policy. You may also be able to bundle your policies together with a single provider to get additional discounts.

Deductibles:

This is true for all insurance plans. They all have deductibles, the lower the deductible the higher the cost. Essentially, deductibles and limits are the ways that insurance companies reduce their risk. The higher the deductible, the more "high frequency, low impact" risk you are assuming, which transforms your policy into more of a "low frequency, high impact" policy.

Playing around with your limits and deductibles can have a significant impact on your overall cost, and benefits provided.

Remember to look at both your short- and long-term financial goals and needs. One of the reasons why the rich get richer is because they can afford to assume certain risks, which allow them to free up short term cash, which helps them make more cash. Juggling which of these competing needs is more important for your long-term success. Similarly, revisiting your policies on a regular basis is critical, we will discuss this further in later chapters.

Agents vs. Brokers

You might be wondering what the difference is between an insurance agent, broker, and advisor. They all work in the same industry and the titles are often used interchangeably. What is the difference?

Agents: many insurance agents typically work with a specific insurance company, if they are only allowed to sell the products of a single company, they are what is called a "captive" agent.

Brokers: Brokers on the other hand, typically represent many different companies, and specialize in helping you shop for different insurance providers, helping you find the best products and prices to match your needs. Within brokers, there may be different types of brokers, with varying access to products. Some brokers may act like captive agents from one or two companies, while others may use specialized software or providers to help them scour dozens of companies to find the right product for you. As your insurance professional what type of agent they are, ask them how many insurance companies they will look at to find the best deal for you and your loved ones. It is the questions we don't ask that often cost us the most.

How to Buy Insurance

Not all insurance companies are created equally. Because of how insurance companies are regulated, insurance companies will choose to favor one type of client over another. This means that depending on your risk demographics, some insurance companies will be more cost effective for you over others.

For instance, there are car insurance companies that specialize in providing coverage for people who have had multiple accidents or lapses in coverage. Conversely, most insurance companies will outright decline those types of clients, or price those types of clients out with exorbitant rates.

It is not that the insurance company is trying to gouge those people, it is just a symptom of how insurance is regulated and how an insurance company needs to be run. If insurance companies took on every risk, they would quickly go bankrupt. Limiting the type of risk and ensuring they are compensated, is how they can provide reasonable coverage for their other clients. However, if you do not match the insurance company's ideal risk profile, then providing coverage is a risky proposition for them.

Shopping around for an insurance company that matches your needs can save you significant amounts of money over time. This is where having a great insurance broker or advisor is critical.

Take the time to shop around, find the best deal for you and your loved ones, don't be afraid to shop around to multiple agents and companies. Take the time to find an agent that you like and who understands your needs. If you're not sure how to find a trustworthy office, ask friends or family members who they recommend or visit sites like Yelp to see reviews of local companies. And always, don't be afraid to ask questions when you don't understand – your agent is there to help! If they cannot explain it to you in a way that you understand, find yourself another agent or broker!

Chapter 8

PLANNING FOR THE INEVITABLE

YOU MAY FEEL THAT you will be forever young, but in the end we all must grow old. Our hair turns grey, our eyesight fades, and it becomes harder to do the things we once found easy. The tale of life is known, there is birth, growth, decline, and death.

if you are going to live the life of your dreams, planning for the march of time is crucial. In this chapter, we are going to talk about how to future proof your financial plan. How do you anticipate your needs for the future, and how do you ensure that your wishes are carried out?

I know this may seem like a daunting task, there are literally countless books written on the subject, each with their own opinion on the best way to accomplish this herculean task. The truth is, planning for the future is quite simple, people who fancy themselves oracles like to make it difficult.

The reality is we can't plan for every eventuality, anybody who says they can predict the future is either a liar or a fool. As Shakespeare writes in Hamlet "there are more things in heaven and earth, Horatio, than are dreamt of in your philosophy." History is littered with examples of people who thought they could predict the future. Leave the fortune telling to the movies. Focus on the eventualities we all know, and the ones that have a high probability of becoming reality.

The following is a list of events that are highly probable or inevitable. These are events that you must account for in your decision-making process, or like hamlet, they will haunt your dreams.

Inflation

Inflation refers to a rise in the average price of goods and services. An example of inflation is if you buy a gallon of milk at the store, and then next year it costs ten cents more than today that is considered inflation.

In 1970, a cup of coffee cost 25 cents, 50 years later that same cup of coffee cost $1.70, almost seven times the cost. It isn't just a cup of coffee, housing, education, electronics, literally everything has increased in price.

How Inflation Has Changed the Price of a Cup of Coffee Over Time

1970	1980	1990	2000	2010	2020
$0.25	$0.45	$0.75	$1.00	$1.25	$1.70

Inflation is a a great thing, it helps stimulate our consumer-based economy. During our working years, inflation is the reason why we continually get job raises, which in turn allows us to borrow money to purchase goods and services. In turn, as the value of money decreases (the reason why goods cost more) we are able to repay our loans with money that is worth less/was easier to earn.

In fact, the Federal Reserve and most Central Banks of the world target a 2% annual inflation rate.

There are several basic causes for inflation: the most basic is supply and demand. When there is more demand than there is supply, then sellers are able to command a higher price for the same goods/services. Sometimes, the cost for raw materials increases, this can be due to scarcity, increased labor costs, increased demand, or a trade war. When the cost for raw goods increase, all the related products increase in price, which eventually can translate to the rest of the economy. All of this economic pressure means that as the cost-of-living increases, workers are able to demand higher wages, which means more pay, and the cycle repeats itself.

How does inflation factor into our financial planning? Inflation means that we have to adjust our long-term goal planning. The further our goal is in the future, the more we will have to adjust it for inflation. It also means that we will have to protect our money from the deteriorating effects of inflation. Just as time wears away at your home, car, and anything that is left out in the elements, money slowly loses its value when left unattended.

How do you protect your money from inflation? There is only one way: **your money needs to make money!**

You need to ensure that your money is growing at least in pace with inflation, preferably faster. Money Market funds used to be designed to keep up with inflation. Unfortunately, The Great Recession really killed that concept. Now, with quantitative easing and the stimulus programs that the Central Banks have been running, government bonds and other "Safe" assets no longer keep pace with inflation.

Today, to protect your assets, you will need to seek alternative safe havens, which we will explore in later chapters of this book.

Aging

Of course, inflation is only one symptom of the test of time. All things age, including our bodies and mind. Like a vintage car, as we age, the cost to maintain our bodies increases.

Injuries take longer to heal, and they can get more expensive, eventually and especially if we are active, our moving parts will need replacing. Knees, hips, and joints in general either need lubrication or replacement with factory fresh parts. Insurance and Medicare will pay for some of the costs, though rarely do they pay for all the costs related to an injury or recovery.

According to Fidelity, the average retiree can expect $295k in medical costs. Medical advances will probably only increase those costs as more lifesaving treatments become available. The good news is that with some planning and foresight you can account for these costs in your planning and ensure that the inevitable challenges of age don't rob your life savings, or fundamentally alter your financial lifestyle.

Long Term Care insurance, Medicare Supplemental Insurance, and Accelerated Death Benefits are just some of the ways you can help transfer some of the financial risks of aging on to others.

Your life insurance policy may allow you to add long-term care or accelerated death benefit riders. These riders may allow you to access part or all of the policies death benefits while still alive. Discuss your options with your financial advisor or insurance broker. These riders and policies vary widely from company to company, shop around and find the best for you and your loved ones. The extra money you pay in premium for the features, far outweighs the costs if you need to use them.

***

Money isn't the only thing we need to consider as we age, Medical Power of Attorney, Living Wills and other documents that let others know how we want to live and be cared for when we are not available or present to express our wishes.

Personally, I highly recommend thinking through these questions and discussing them with your significant other. If you have them in writing, ensure that your emergency contacts are aware of your wishes so, they can advocate for you, if and when you need them.

In the last few days of my dad's life, his bones were riddled with painful cancer, he needed painkillers but kept saying his pain was a 4 out of 6. When the nurses would leave, he would turn to me and say, "I've never been in more pain in my life." He turned down painkillers out of habit, he was a child of the 60s, and experimented as a teenager and young adult. After he became sober, he did his best to avoid heavy painkillers. My dad needed someone else to make the choices for him, but he had not taken the time to appoint a Medical Power of Attorney or write a Living Will, if he had, he would not have needed to suffer as much as he did in those final days. It is easy to say that this will not happen to you. Please take a few minutes and ensure that it does not happen to you. There are free sites where you can craft these documents online.

On the same note as Medical Power of Attorneys, you should create a durable power of Attorney.

A Durable Power of Attorney allows you to specify that an individual or individual can act on your behalf, in limited (or unlimited) situations, when certain circumstances occur. For instance, in the event of a person's incapacitation for an extended period. I knew an Advisor whose family lost their business because his dad was in a car accident and creditors were able to liquidate the business, because he was the only one authorized to pay his company's bills.

Power of Attorneys and Living Wills are simple and easy to create documents that can help you protect yourself and your loved ones. At a minimum, ensure that if you are not available to answer questions for a few weeks or months that your finances won't be devastated because bills were not paid, or because your loved ones didn't know to pay them, or were not authorized to pay them.

Survivorship Planning

My wife and I have a deal, or rather I should say she has a deal, and I don't have a choice. The deal is that she dies first, because as she puts it, "I can't live without you, so I have to die first." If only life were so cooperative, maybe this book is my insurance against my untimely demise :-)

Planning for the inevitable and what happens next is important and it is incredibly easy; when you are cognizant of the importance of planning for the inevitable.

Death rarely happens the way we picture it, the movies portray death as an "event." Financial Advisors talk about it, but few have experienced what happens after someone dies. The emotions, the millions and one little decision that needs to be made, and the complete chaos that surrounds death. The proverb about battleplans not surviving contact with the enemy is doubly true for death. Death is not an orderly affair – unless you take the time to plan for it.

The good news is that as part of this book, we will develop the financial habits so, that planning for death does not become an overwhelming and time-consuming task. If we are smart, organized, and we make others aware of our wishes, death does not have to bring about financial ruin and chaos.

In this section, we are going to focus on the financial changes that happen after death, and how to minimize their impact. Please note the following is general in nature, I do not make any claims as the accuracy of this information or how it applies to you and your jurisdiction. Please take some time and consult with estate attorney for details on how this works in your locale.

Generally speaking, at some point, shortly after the death certificate is filed with the local jurisdiction, government agencies and registrars are notified. This notification will trigger a freeze on any bank accounts or credit cards that are held in the deceased person's name. In practical terms, this means that any automatic payments that are coming from those accounts will get rejected and late fees will get assessed. I would recommend that utilities and other essential expenses be paid out of joint titled accounts.

How an account is "titled" determines who owns the account, and more importantly how funds are distributed in the event of their death. In addition to the "titling" of the account, there are what are known as "pay-on-death", "transfer-on-death", or "beneficiary" forms that can determine how the account is distributed after death.

Contrary to what many people think, a will, trust, or other contracts do **NOT** dictate what happens with these accounts. The reason for why this is so, has to do with the technicalities of the law and the timing of the contracts. The end result is that in case after case, the courts have ruled in favor of the bank's instructions over wills or other written instructions. This little fact has cost people hundreds of thousands of dollars. Oftentimes people will forget to update their 401k or work benefits and their ex-spouse will still be listed as the beneficiary of their accounts.

My dad, when he was first diagnosed with cancer, started the process of updating his beneficiary forms, and when he died, we discovered a beneficiary form that he had signed and dated, but had not submitted to HR. HR said they would accept the update in the beneficiary form, but they needed the original. By the time they had received the original form, Vanguard who was the actual custodian of the account and benefits, had already paid out his 401k and filed the paperwork with his group's life insurance policy.

Bottom line: always make sure that you have a beneficiary listed and make sure to keep it current. One advantage of having a beneficiary listed is that your account does not need to go to Probate, allowing your beneficiaries to access your funds almost instantly.

Probate is a legal process, which requires an executor to be assigned by the court, which requires a court date and filings, and can take time and money. It also means waiting for a death certificate which can sometimes take weeks to be issued, especially if there are unusual circumstances, or you have the misfortune of dying in a US territory like Washington DC.

Additionally, not everything can be transferred on death, things like Wages, or Social Security/Pension Benefits are tied to a specific individual, what happens to that income once the beneficiary passes? How will their significant other replace that income? These are questions you need to think through, the answers to these questions may alter your financial plans or cause you to purchase additional life insurance or specify how your life insurance proceeds are used.

When evaluating Financial Decisions, you need to think about the long-term consequences, how will this decision affect me now, how will it affect me in the future, and how will it affect my loved ones after I die. If you get into the habit of asking those questions each time you make a financial decision, you will eventually create a financial cushion for your loved ones, so that when life does not go the way you plan, at least there will be enough "right things" to keep your financial ship steady and on course.

In the next chapter we are going to discuss how to build a financial moat of goodness that protects us from bad or incorrect financial decisions.

Chapter 9

CAPTURING UPSIDE

T HE READER'S DIGEST RECENTLY did a piece called "Internet Hacks that Just Don't Work." As part of the piece, they asked industry experts what are some of the myths and misconceptions that people have that simply were not true. Here was my response, which they featured in their issue:

Myth: Giving up your daily Starbucks will make you a millionaire

Giving up a small, daily luxury—like a coffee or a bagel—is one of the most commonly shared financial "hacks." The idea is that little savings add up to big bucks over time. However, this isn't enough for most people, says Leibel Sternbach, a financial advisor and the founder of Yields4U.com. "This hack is so harmful; words can't even begin to describe the amount of damage this does to people. No matter how much you manage to save by cutting your expenses, the fact is that for most people, adding an extra $500 or $1,000 to your savings a year isn't going to make you be able to magically retire," he says. "Before you start cutting expenses, figure out how to invest in your earning potential. Increasing your salary will exponentially increase the amount you can save by far more than cutting out your daily Starbucks."

As much as we would like to think, and as much as we feel, that "saving" and "protecting" our money is what we need to do to retire - the reality is that we need our money to grow.

Realistically most people will not earn enough money to retire. The only way to transform our savings into a sum of money that is sufficient to achieve our goals, is by putting our money to work, by making our money grow into more money.

In this chapter, we are going to explore the basic methods for growing your money. The pros and cons of each method, and how to protect your financial freedom and your goals while you are investing.

Was to Grow Your Money

There are only two ways to grow your money: you can either loan your money to someone, or you can invest in something that will either increase in value, return profits, or ideally both. All other ways of earning money are forms of speculation, aka gambling.

The world would have you believe that there are thousands of ways to grow your money. However, if you look closer at the details, you will discover that all opportunities fall into one of these three categories. It is important to keep this in mind as we explore various investment options.

Loans:

When we loan money to people, we are taking on a risk that our money will not be returned. In *return* for that risk, we will be paid interest. The greater the risk of loss, the more interest we can demand.

This risk/reward relationship can help explain why it is easier for rich people to get loans, the risk of them defaulting on their loans is much lower. This dynamic also explains why secured loans, i.e., loans where the creditor can sell property to collect their loan, like a mortgage, have lower interest rates than credit cards, after all, the lender is only risking the cost of collecting and selling your property, and not their entire principal.

Loans can take on many different forms, and sometimes investments can masquerade as loans, such as payday loans, or 0% financing loans. In these transactions, the lender is more interested in earning interest than in recovering their principal, as such they are not really loans and much as investments. I talk more about this in previous chapters where I talk about good debt vs. bad debt.

Investments:

A good description of an investment is a purchase that you expect will appreciate in value, produce income, or provide some other financial benefit. Some examples of investments are:

- A home that you hope will increase in value
- Rental property that will produce income
- Paying for an education to earn more money
- Paying to Learn new skills to be able to earn more
- Buying goods at wholesale to sell individually
- Investing in starting a business
- Investing in other people's businesses

Of course, you don't need to be the person to do the actual buying or selling, you could always hire someone else to do all the heavy lifting for you.

In starting a business there is usually one party who provides the money and another who does all the heavy lifting, typically the money person is known as a "silent investor." In exchange for their money, the silent investor may get "**preferred**" treatment, this can mean that when profits are taken, they get paid first, or in the event of a bankruptcy, they have a higher claim to the company's assets than the other partners. This would be in contrast to the **common** owners of the company.

There are many different types of companies, some are Limited Liability Companies or Partnerships, others are Incorporated (inc.) The primary difference is that companies that are incorporated must issue **shares** or **stock** in their company, while owners in a Limited Liability Companies own the proportional share of the company based on their operating agreement and tax basis in the company.

As a business generates revenue, buys goods and properties, and grows in value; it builds equity. This equity is similar to the equity in your home, the business can borrow against the equity, and at sale, the equity in the business generally has more value than its other assets.

As you are probably aware, there are not very many people who are in the **market** to buy **private equity.** It is called **private**, because it is not available on the open market. By law, these companies are not allowed to solicit investments from the general public, unless they are **public** companies.

Public companies are regulated by the government, there are rules about how they must behave, and the transparency they need to provide to the public. There are serious limitations on what they can do, and how they can operate. In exchange for these restrictions, which are designed to protect the public good, they are allowed to borrow and sell ownership stakes to the general public.

There are many different types of companies, most companies specialize in doing one thing really well, McDonalds sells fast food, Starbucks sells coffee, **Mutual Funds** are a type of company that specializes in managing investments. **Mutual Funds** are run like any other company, they have a board of directors, which hires a CEO or **Investment Manager.** Similar to other companies, the board determines what the company should do, and the company uses its resources and skills to make a profit, which are then **distributed** to their owners or **shareholders.** Typically, companies will distribute to their owners a portion of a **dividends**[1] of their profits. **Dividends** can be in the form of Cash or Stock in the company.

Mutual Funds are also known as **Open Ended Funds**, this is because unlike a traditional company which has a limited number of stocks or shares, a Mutual Fund has the special ability to issue an unlimited number of new shares.

The number of shares a Mutual Fund has can fluctuate each day, and like any other company, Mutual Funds can become insolvent and go out of business. Since the number of **outstanding shares** or shares held by the public can fluctuate, and since these companies are specifically designed to manage investments, regulators require that **Mutual Funds** publish the daily equity or investment value of each share, this number is called the **Net Asset Value or NAV.**

It is important to know, when a **Mutual Fund** goes bankrupt, or is in the process of shutting down, or when they feel that owners liquidating their shares will hurt other investors in the company - the **Mutual Fund** can limit or halt all liquidations/withdrawals until a time of their choosing.

The combinations and permutations of companies and investment companies that you can conjure up are endless. I could dedicate a thousand pages to describing all the different vehicles available today - and tomorrow there would be three more to add to the list.

The important takeaway is that there really are only three ways to make money: loan it, invest it in yourself, use it to

---

1   According to the Oxford Dictionary a dividend is a number to be divided by another number.

buy ownership/equity in a property or company, or speculate/ gamble on the future.

Getting the Biggest Bang for Your Buck

When we objectively look at the returns, we could potentially get on our investment of time and money, the following should become obvious:

Build Your Freedom Fund

It goes without saying, your financial freedom comes first, everything else comes second. The more financial freedom you have, the greater your ability to make smarter decisions for yourself and your loved ones. Additionally, by having a financial freedom fund, you will have a pot of money that you could use to take advantage of once in a lifetime opportunity that would otherwise pass you by.

Paying Off High Interest Credit Cards

Paying down high interest loans and credit cards are like a guaranteed return on your investment. For every dollar you pay down it is an instant #% return on your investment. This only applies to interest rates, which are significantly higher than the returns you could get by investing your money. Keep in mind, saving on interest is virtually guaranteed, while investment returns are not.

Investing in Your Ability to Earn a Higher Wage

Wages are the ultimate form of compounding interest. Remember any future increases in your salary will be based on your *current* wages. The earlier in life that you increase your salary, the longer you will have for it to compound and product a greater return. Invest in your education - to the extent that it will increase your salary. Get certifications, designations and advance your professional education as much as possible. Not only will this increase the wages you earn, but it can increase your Social Security benefits during retirement.[2]

Max Out Your Employer Retirement Contributions

If your employer offers matching contributions to your retirement account - take them up on their offer. Max it out. Dollar for dollar, matching contributions are a guaranteed return on your investment. You will be hard pressed to find a better opportunity.

Equities

For the average investor, who do not have access or the financial ability to invest in private equity, investing in companies, either directly or indirectly, will provide the next highest return.

Loans, Bonds, Notes, and Treasuries

All of these investments are different forms of loans to companies, organizations or governments. The risks associated with the loan will generally determine the type of interest that is offered.

In theory, there is an inherent security in loans, primarily that your principal will be returned to you after a short(ish)

---

2   There is a cap to Social Security Benefits, so at a certain point higher wages may not contribute to additional retirement benefits.

period of time. Contrast this risk with that of a stock, which you have no contractual guarantee of getting your principal returned. Of course, if the company goes bankrupt you loan is unlikely to return it's full principal, and your money can be tied up for years as the company works through bankruptcy.

There was a time when "safe" bonds, ie bonds for companies like IBM, paid decent interest rates, and were a viable alternative to the risks associated with equities. This has not been true since at least The Great Recession and is unlikely to be true anytime soon.

Mortgages:

Just a quick note, there is a misconception that paying off your mortgage early is beneficial and should be done shortly after paying off credit cards. This is one of those conventional wisdoms that no longer holds true.

There were times when interest rates were higher and market returns were significantly lower. Additionally, many investment options used to be harder to access, costly, if not impossible to access. Today, thanks to the internet and startups like Robinhood, any investor has access to almost every investment vehicle, commission free, and with the swipe of a finger. With cost and access restrictions eliminated, and tax benefits modified, paying off your mortgage is one of those conventional wisdoms that no longer hold up to the test of time.

Additionally, as The Great Recession taught many investors, just because you have equity in your home today - does not mean it will be there tomorrow, or that you will be able to access it when you need it. Markets and other investments have a lot more liquidity than your home equity.

Your home is a single asset, as the old saying goes, don't put all your eggs in a single basket. This is doubly true for your investments. Don't put all your life savings into a single asset that is difficult and expensive to sell or borrow against, it just doesn't make any sense. Obviously, circumstances change, and everyone's situation is different, so use *The 5-Minute Planning* process to evaluate your decisions, and determine what is the best course of action for you and your loved ones.

***

Investing is no longer optional!

In the last section we covered the basic vehicles available to everyone to grow their money. You may be wondering why you would need to invest your money, and why "safe" options, such as Bank CDs or Bonds, are no longer sufficient. There was a time when savings accounts and Bank CDs (Certificate of Deposits) provided adequate growth. There was a time when most people could combine the equity in their home, the growth of their savings, with their pension or 401k, and social security and they would have enough money to live out their golden years.

In fact, my first "retirement" plan was to accumulate enough wealth so that I could live off the interest that my money would earn in a high yields savings account or Bank CD - this was back in the day when 5% interest was possible. It has been over a decade since I have seen 5% yields on Bank

CDs, and savings accounts have just started edging over 1% - and this is at the fringe, online only banks.

As individuals, the days of being able to let your money sit on the sidelines are long gone. Today, if your money isn't actively growing, and growing at a steady clip, then you are going backwards. The old saying about business, "if you aren't growing then you are dying" applies to your money.

Money is a tool, fundamentally, money is a replacement for time. We exchange our time for money, and in return we pay other people for their time and money. We pay the grocery store, who pays the farmer to grow his crops, we pay our plumbers and our electricians, money is literally a measure of the value of time. Time and energy are the only things we cannot create or destroy.

Considering this view of money, let me pose a question: if you had all the time in the world, would you choose to do nothing with your time? Probably not! I am sure you have goals for your retirement, things you want to do, goals you would like to accomplish.

Stop thinking of your money as a piece of furniture, it is little copies of you sitting in a vault, waiting to be activated and put to work. You could store those little pieces of you, for later, for times when you don't have the time or energy - or you could put it to work creating more time/money for you!

Your Money Needs to Make You Money!

Having accepted the reality that your money needs to grow, and become more money, especially in light of the fact that time and inflation will slowly erode your money's value. The question is how do we grow our money in a way that does not undermine our overall financial security, or unnecessarily delay the realization of our goals?

I don't have a magic bullet for you, a cure-all that will guarantee success without failure. What I can offer you is a process that will help increase your probability of success while protecting your downside as much as possible.

As you have gone through this process of creating your *5-Minute Plan*, you should have clarity as to what you need financially and emotionally in order to feel secure. Once you have that in place, the next step is to create an investment plan that will grow your money with confidence and peace of mind.

The creation of an investment plan is well beyond the scope of this book. In this book, I will provide you with an outline of the framework and the questions you need to answer in order to have a solid plan. If you want a step-by-step guide on how to build and run your investment plan, check out my next book on investing.

How to Invest Successfully
Have an Evidence Based Investment Plan!

As we have discussed throughout this book, as human beings we are emotional creatures. Nature has evolved our instincts to protect us and ensure the continued survival of our species. All the traits that allow us to dominate the food chain, and outlast every other species, are the same characteristics that make us terrible with money.

There are many reasons why people fail to make good financial decisions. In fact, the DALBAR institute has conducted a yearly study of investors. The study has constantly found that the "average" investor has underperformed the market, usually by wide margins - and the reasons are consistent; human nature, when unregulated, leads to poor investment choices.

In response to these studies, the media, and the financial pornography industry has touted headline grabbing advice such as "buy and hold," or "value investing" or "low-cost indexing." These strategies, when implemented without proper thought or consideration, are no better than picking your investments by rolling a dice, throwing darts, or consulting your local fortune teller.

In order for an investment strategy to work, it needs to be rules based, it needs to be a repeatable process, it needs to be grounded in facts and logic, it needs to be based on evidence, and it needs to adapt to changing environments. Investing without a plan is no different than gambling.

A Plan Based on Facts and Not "Hopes & Prayers"

There is a fundamental truth about investing that every successful investor knows. Failure is inevitable! The question isn't will you fail, but how often will you fail, and will your failures decimate your life savings, or will you be able to recover?

Investing without a plan is scary, it is no different than going to Vegas and betting your rent money. There was a period of time, when my dad was obsessed with Blackjack. I think it was shortly after he lost all his money in the stock market. My dad became convinced that there was a way to beat the casinos at Blackjack. He bought this trading system and software that would teach you how to predict the cards. The core of the strategy was that when the odds were not in your favor you bet small amounts, and when the odds were in your favor your bet larger amounts, thus allowing you to beat the house at their own game. It is a nice theory, it might even work, he was never successful with it, he lost his shirt quite a few times trying.

If only my dad had applied, his Blackjack strategy to the markets - he would have been wildly successful. Unlike casinos, the stock market is fair game. The odds of you winning can be stacked in your favor. In fact, you don't even need to play the game to win, you just need to buy-in and wait. Since 1920, the market has returned an inflation adjusted average annual return of 7.61% a year. Of course, there were periods of extreme loss, like the Great Depression, WWII, the 70s, Black Monday, etc...

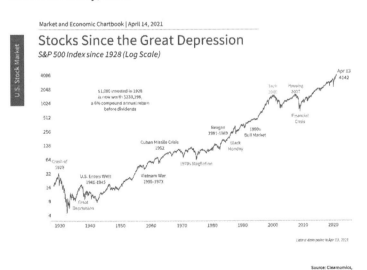

As we have covered previously, the reason why most financial plans fail is because emotions and finances do not mix well together. When investing, it is easy to get scared and sell at the wrong times or get caught up in the excitement and buy at the wrong time or for the wrong reasons. Hopefully, you will have established a freedom fund, one that will protect your essentials and lifestyle should everything fail.

Once you have your bottom line covered, you can then afford to invest for the long run, you can afford to invest money and ignore your investment for a year, two years or even ten years! Your financial and emotional happiness is no longer tied to the outcome of a specific investment because you have protected yourself.

So, let us talk about some basic rules of investing, rules that hold true regardless of the economy, regardless of changes in technology, these are fundamental truths that will remain as long as markets are free and founded on capitalism.

Truth: Equity Markets Will Always Increase

There are hundreds of books written on this subject, and there is an entire field of study called economics, which tries to explain how and why economies work. The reality is that as long as the world population and as long as the world continues to provide a way for companies to profit, i.e. we don't suddenly all become socialists, the aggregate value of all these companies will only increase, and as long as these companies remain publicly traded then you, as an investor, will have access to participate in the growth.

Another way to think of it, is you are loaning or investing in the companies that turn around and hire you, pay you wages, so that you can in turn buy their products and services. Henry Ford was the first CEO to realize this reality, and it is why he built company towns, and why he gave his workers off on Saturday. Ford didn't do it because he was generous, he did it because it gave his workers an opportunity to spend their wages at his company owned stores and on his products. This cycle of consumerism is unlikely to end anytime soon.

You can choose to "hold" on to your money. However, unless you are sticking your money in the freezer, by putting your money in the bank, all you are doing is giving the banks the right to use your money without paying a fee. Savings accounts pay a small amount of interest in exchange for holding on to your money for longer, Bank Certificate of Deposits, are essentially savings accounts that you can't touch for longer periods of time. Of course, you can "loan" your money to companies other than banks, in doing this you increase your risk. The more concentrated your risk the greater the potential reward.

Truth: Diversification Reduces Risk

Continuing with our loans example, when you give your money to the bank, the bank in turn will use your cash, or loan it out to borrowers. Banks reduce their risk of any one loan going bad, by loaning to multiple people, this way if one loan goes bad, they still have others that will pay sufficient interest to cover the losses.

it goes without saying that this is an oversimplification. In reality, banks don't even hold on to the loans, in fact they further divide up the loans and then sell bundles of **diversified** pieces of loans back to other banks or the public. These loans are sold as bonds, notes, or other **securities.**

This process is known as **Securitization**, and the instruments created are called **derivatives**, because they derive their value from the value of something else, i.e. the loans and the interest paid on these loans. Many of these bundles of loans are then used as part of retirement portfolios; because the interest they pay is used as retirement income by many investors.

Just as banks reduce their risk of any one loan going bad, you as an investor can also diversify your investments. For example, if you invest in a single pizza store, you have a lot of risk concentrated in that pizza store. However, if you invest in 100 pizza stores, your risk of any single store failing is much lower. Of course, if suddenly the government started taxing pizza, or it was discovered that pizza caused cancer, you would probably face a terrible loss. You can diversify against this danger by spreading your money, you could invest not just in pizza shops, but salad bars as well. An event that would cause people to stop visiting pizza shops is unlikely to affect the profitability of a salad bar - unless that event is **systemic**, like a pandemic that causes a disruption to the entire system.

One of the reasons why people hate investing is because systemic events happen, and while statistically they aren't supposed to be frequent - they happen a lot more than statistics dictate. Just in my lifetime, we had a world power default on their debt ('87), the dot com bust of '00-02, we had the Great Recession ('07-'09), the COVID-19 pandemic, and we have had multiple, once in a century storms like hurricane Katrina, Harvey, winter storm Nemo, and many others that have caused billions in damages.

Diversification Methods

There are three basic methods that the average investor has taken to protecting themselves from the risks associated with **systemic** type events. There are others, but they are beyond the scope of this book.

Diversification Method #1: Accepting the Risk

One of the reasons why finding good investment advice is hard, is because what constitutes good advice for one person may, be terrible for another.

For instance, a person that is at the peak of their career, and they have 20+ years until retirement, for them accepting the risks of a black swan event, such as The Great Recession, is probably the right decision. Working people are probably contributing to their savings on a regular basis, and because they don't need their money any time soon, these down markets can provide quite a boost to their net worth, at least over time.

When you are regularly adding new money to your investments, what ends up happening is that some of your money will invest at the lows of the market and some at the heights of the market, which means on average you will be investing at the middle of the market. Let that sink in for a second.

The goal of investing is to buy low and sell high, investing in this manner, of contributing amounts over time, allows you to achieve the next best thing – on autopilot. Genius! Of course, this only works if you have a separate financial freedom fund setup, so that you don't need to touch your investments during these down years. Withdrawing funds during down years will cause you to accelerate your losses and lengthen your recovery, which is what happened to many people after the dotcom bust, and The Great Recession.

Diversification Method #2: Taming the Wave

The second method is what I like to call Taming the Wave. This is usually practiced by people who need access to their savings, or rely on their savings for income, or just don't have the time to allow their portfolios to recover from a major loss.

In Taming the Wave method, we accept that black swan events will happen. Instead of trying to avoid the waves, we learn to tame and ride the waves in a way that does not adversely affect our financial success.

There are several investing techniques that are built around this principle, fundamentally they require a good freedom fund, and then stratifying, banding, or bucketing your investments over your time horizon.

The core principle is diversifying your risk levels based on the timeframe for needing access to your funds. Your near-term funds carry less risk than your long-term money, allowing more of your money to weather market storms and capture the market's long-term growth.

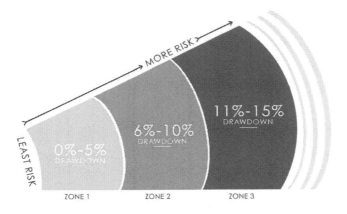

There are a lot of ways to achieve the benefits of this type of diversification including: time banding, bucketing, core and satellite, and income-based strategies to name just a few. I will go into the details of each strategy in my next book on investing.

Method #3: Swapping Risks

The third method for reducing systemic risk is through transference. If you remember, in the last few chapters, we discussed how insurance is a way to transfer risk, a similar concept exists in the investment world.

In the investment world, there are numerous methods for transferring risk. Historically, these tools were unavailable to the average investor. Today, with the wave of democratization that is happening in finance, more and more of these tools are available today. Here are some of the types of tools.

Options, Futures, Swaps and Forward Contracts: Fundamentally these are contracts where one person agrees to buy or sell something at a specified rate, in exchange they either pay a premium or earn a premium. One way to think of this is like going into a contract on a home, the buyer agrees to buy the house on or before a specified date for a specified price. In exchange for this right, the buyer pays a non-refundable fee.

Typically, contracts to buy a piece of property are non-transferable, meaning, the buyer can't sell their "contract" to another buyer. Investments on the other hand are transferable, which means there is an entire market built around the trading of these contracts.

These contracts can be used to buy/sell specific securities, these are typically **options.** They could also be used to buy real assets like corn, lumber and oil, these are typically called **Commodity Futures, or Commodities** for short.

You can also get creative, and instead of buying or selling, you can trade or **swap** two assets – or two values, sometimes arbitrary values. If you think that sounds like gambling, you are not alone. When the first commodities exchange was created, they had to have a specific carveout written into the existing gambling laws that excluded these types of contracts, otherwise they would be illegal under existing gambling laws.

So, what do all these options do for you? They give you the ability to participate in the markets without assuming their full risk. For example, you can buy what is called an Equity or Market Linked CD. This is a certificate of deposit, except instead of paying a flat interest rate, it pays you a rate that is a percentage of the market gains for a particular market or group of securities, also known as an **Index.**

Lately, there has been the proliferation of **Exchange Traded Notes or ETNs**, these notes, or loans, act as if they have embedded swap or forward type contracts. These contracts are used to determine the amount of interest the note will pay.

A notes rate can be based on the lessor performance of say the S&P 500 or the Nasdaq 1000, or really any two indexes, or a percentage of an index, up to a max percentage or **ceiling**. They may even protect your downside by absorbing a limited amount of loss, providing a **buffer** to your investment. They might also protect against catastrophic losses by setting a **Floor,** or maximum loss to your investment. Ordinarily investments cannot guarantee against loss, in this case they are not guaranteeing your principal, rather the contract relates to the amount of interest you will earn or lose.

Also, unlike a forward or swap contract, since these are exchange traded that means you can sell it on the open market and exit your position anytime, which is a definite positive over ordinary forward contracts.

Swapping Risks Through Insurance: As we have discussed in earlier chapters, insurance is a means for transferring risk from one party to another. Insurance companies, not wanting to be left out of the gold rush happening to the markets during the 90s, started offering Equity linked contracts, these generally come in the form of Equity Indexed Universal Life Contracts, and Variable- and Fixed-Indexed Annuities. I won't go into the full details of either of these contracts in this book, I do discuss them in detail in my next book on retirement.

The short version, is that insurance companies offer policies that accumulate value based on the performance of one or more market indexes, since life insurance and annuity products are typically used to provide retirement income or death benefits, the contracts are simpler, and generally will provide a 0% floor, so in years where the market has a loss, you won't lose any of your **accumulated** "value." However, in years where the market has gains, your upside will be limited by a **cap** or **ceiling** and a **participation rate**, i.e. You will only **participate** in 35% of the market's growth, or whatever the rate your contract specifies.

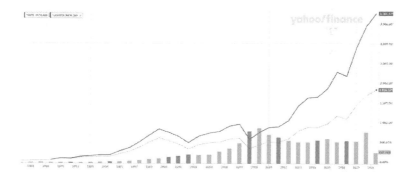

Additionally, the index that is used is the **price index** and not the **total return index.** The price of a security might only go from $1 to $1.10, a modest 10% gain, however the security could have paid a dividend of 10% as well, which would bring your total return, closer to 20%. From 1986 to 2021 about 51% of market returns could be attributed to dividends. In addition to limiting your market participation by a percentage, they are also choosing indexes that are not a true reflection of an investor's performance.

The true value of these policies is in their insurance benefits, not their market benefits. If the goal of your investment is to be converted into retirement income, or to provide your spouse and loved ones with a death benefit, or if you have a large amount of taxable income that you would like to grow tax deferred/tax-free, then life insurance can provide some very appealing options.

Remember, insurance is about transferring risk. Annuity policies provide a "lifetime income" benefit to one or more beneficiaries. In exchange for premium payments and the time value of your money, insurance companies will assume the risk of growing your assets/you outlive your assets and agree to pay you a predetermined amount of money for as long as you, and/or your spouse live. This can be a great deal for some people, and a terrible deal for others.

It is worth nothing that Social Security is a government mandated and run Annuity contract, which you already own and pay into. Insurance companies offer a private version, with quite a bit more options, and is regulated for your benefit; unlike Social Security which is continually robbed by congress for their benefit.

Truth: Risk Cannot Be Eliminated, Only Transformed

Based on all the information you have learned so far, it would be easy to assume that there was a magic bullet for eliminating or hedging risk. The financial pornography industry is full of claims that would lead you to believe that you are just one strategy away from certain wealth or guaranteed performance. The reality, similar to the law of physics regarding energy, is that risk cannot be eliminated. Risk can only be transferred or transformed. We can exchange one risk, for another risk, we can change the type of risks we are assuming; however, there is no way to entirely eliminate risk. The trick is to build a strategy that minimizes your risk as much as *necessary*, but no more. The more risk you eliminate, the less upside you are likely to experience. If you have a good understanding of your physical and emotional needs, and you have a good financial freedom fund, then you should be able to easily answer how much risk aversion is necessary in order for you to feel confident in your financial choices.

Creating Your Investment Plan

Take a second to think about all the lessons you have learned in this book. We started down this journey by realizing that human beings are ill designed for making sound financial decisions. Our solution, *The 5-Minute Plan* solution is to insulate and separate ourselves emotionally and financially from our financial decisions. By insulating ourselves from our decisions, we allow ourselves to step back and make rational choices. The only way to do this is to protect our bottom line. Everything in this book has been about helping you define what your bottom line is, both emotionally and financially. Investments are no different.

To create a sound investment strategy, you need to first understand what your bottom line is. What are the triggers that will cause you to hate your choices, and what are the triggers that will force you emotionally to make bad investment decisions?

No matter how great you are, unless you are a sociopath, there will be a point where the emotional pain of experiencing the market's volatility, those wild swings up and down, will get to you. Know yourself, know where those points are, and if you don't know where those points are, watch and learn as you experience them over time so you can avoid them in the future. A good advisor will help you identify and navigate those events.

Once you know what your bottom line is, ask yourself, where do you want to go? What are your goals? What are the investment options that can help you get to your goals, while still honoring your emotional needs?

You may find that you need to pull back on your expectations, or you may find emotional resolve in the desire to achieve your goals, resolve that helps you overcome your insecurities and anxieties. Remember, as long as you are diversified, meaning you've minimized the dangers from any single company, sector, or market; you now have the ability to capture the markets long term, upward trend. You just need to be able to hold on for the ride!

How can you hold on to the ride when it becomes volatile? Choose one of the diversification methods we discussed, find the combination that provides the ride you are comfortable with, and then go back to your life, let time do its thing. If you don't know what that investment plan looks like, if you don't know where to begin, go buy my next book on investing. in it I discuss specifics of how to build, or outsource, investment strategies that will fit your financial and emotional needs.

Chapter 10

WEATHERING TURBULENCE

LIFE WOULD BE BORING if it followed a straight path. There are bumps, potholes, and obstacles in our way that make this journey interesting. How we react to life's challenges determines the quality of our lives. In many ways, life is like a giant road trip, with hills and valleys, long stretches of flat roads, and sometimes even treacherous mountain passes.

We all have periods where things go well, no problems or crises to deal with, and then there are stretches where we feel like the whole world is crashing down on us. Greatness and inner peace come from learning how to weather turbulence, not run away from it.

We cannot control the things that happen outside our immediate sphere. We cannot change how the markets behave, or what congress will do next. What we can do is control our reactions. If this sounds familiar, it should. This is the life lesson we all learn in life; we cannot control others, only how we react. When it comes to our finances, it is no different.

The moment you realize that there are things outside your immediate sphere of influence, and you accept them as they currently exist, you will feel liberated. You will have nothing left to worry about. How much money am I going to make? What investments will pay off? How long before my business takes off? We are not really sure what is around the next bend of the road so, let go of any expectations or predictions. Enjoy where each day leads you, because we don't know what tomorrow might bring.

So, how do you enjoy the moment, and ride the wave, when your financial future is at stake? In my experience, the same methodology that applies to a road trip, to a vacation, relationships, apply to finance as well. Here are my rules for surviving life.

Surviving Life - Step #1: Protect Yourself

You cannot be a good spouse, parent, partner, or person unless you first take care of your emotional and physical needs. There is a reason why the safety instructions on a plan are to put on your oxygen mask first, then help your kids. If you are unconscious, if you are drowning, you cannot help anyone else - including yourself.

In the first chapter, we built our emergency fund, our financial freedom fund, your You Only Live Once (YOLO) fund. This is our safety net; this is your cushion. If and when everything goes pear-shaped, belly up, if the worst happens, our freedom fund will help us get back on our feet. Protecting yourself and your bottom line is the first step in overcoming life's obstacles.

Surviving Life - Step #2: Set Checkpoints

In the days before GPS, you would map out your road trip. You would set checkpoints, take highway x to exit y, stop at town z for lunch.

There will be times when life throws you curveballs; a layoff, a career change, a divorce, there will be times when we don't know what comes next. Protect your sanity, protect your decision-making abilities, and remind yourself that these are just bumps in the road. We will overcome these bumps and challenges, live will continue onwards, as long as we set checkpoints for ourselves.

Checkpoints are times and events that will trigger us to reevaluate our plan. It can be when you do taxes, or maybe after New Year's, or it could be when certain events take place, such as a change in employment, a change in health, something that would fundamentally alter the assumptions we base our decisions on.

For example, there was a time when my only goal was to save enough money to buy a Dodge Charger. At some point in my life, my goal changed. I met the love of my life, and a wedding ring became a more important goal. Once I was married, owning a car was no longer as important as leasing a car, it was something that was really important to my wife and in-laws. I never did end up buying that Dodge Charger. If I had continued blindly, I would have made many incorrect financial choices, based on bad information and assumptions. How much time and frustration would I have encountered, working towards a goal that I no longer desired?

Set up checkpoints for yourself, they should be both time and event. If you make this a habit, it will become second nature to you. Think of these checkpoints as reality checks. Are my assumptions still true? Did events pan out the way I expected? Do I need to change my actions based on what life is telling me?

The more we incorporate this behavior into our lives, the closer we will be able to bring our current reality to our goals and ideal reality.

As Carl Richards, a New York Times best-selling author and financial columnist likes to say, the job of a planner is to narrow the possible outcomes. The more we re-evaluate, the more we correct our course, the closer we will get to our target destination.

Just a note, you don't want to over-check or over-correct, finding a balance is challenge of life, and how often, and how much to course correct, is really a personal decision. As the Marines say "Preserve, Adapt, and Overcome!" A good financial advisor will help keep you in check and on track for your goals.

Surviving Life Step #3: Adapt & Overcome

When challenges arise, don't allow them to dictate who you are, or where your life is headed. Remind yourself of all the successes in the past, know that you have taken the steps to protect your bottom line, so your worst-case scenarios are protected. Your choice now, is how do you adapt and overcome the current obstacle that life has thrown in your path.

Let us take a truly devastating scenario, it is 2008, you were planning on selling your home and retiring to Florida, suddenly, the banks stop giving out mortgages and your home value drops by 40%. You cannot sell your home, and you can't buy your new home. And to make matters worse, you were counting on part of the proceeds of the sale to fund part of your retirement.

At this point, there really is nothing you can do. You could beat yourself up, berate yourself for not selling your home earlier - but there really was no good financial reason to sell earlier. Also, you cannot change the past. What you can do is learn from life's lessons and move on. In this case, it means maybe re-evaluating when you move to Florida, or it may mean renting out your home until property values recover.

Alternatively, you could view it as an opportunity to buy your dream property in Florida at a discount. If you had a good financial freedom fund, you would probably have the money to be able to secure the property for yourself. In this way, you would be able to both benefit from the housing bust and the recovery, by buying your new house low and selling your current home when the market returns to normal levels.

Of course, if you are strapped for cash, these options would not be available to you. You would be forced to sell your house at the worst possible time or live in your home longer. The option to rent out your home would not be possible, because you did not have the resources to be able to take advantage of the opportunities available.

As I am sure you can see, when you have a financial freedom fund, when you have a financial decision-making process, when you have confidence in your ability to persevere, adapt and overcome - life becomes a lot more enjoyable.

To drive my point home, I would like to share two stories. Both are the same story, they both happened to me and my wife, the feeling and experiences could not have been more different.

When we first got married, on one of our drive homes from Cleveland (a 500-mile drive) we ran out of gas. It was 3 o'clock in the morning, on I-80, in the middle of nowhere Pennsylvania, on a major, two-lane trucking route - with no streetlights. We called AAA, and ended up spending a bit over an hour, under the stars, having a romantic time together.

Fast forward 8-years later, myself, my wife, and child were driving back from an alligator farm in Florida, and as the gas light went on, my wife started navigating me to a gas station. About 15 minutes into her navigation, I am getting nervous as hell, traffic is coming to a stall, and we are still on the highway. I ask my wife how far the gas station is, "11 miles", she says.

I start freaking out, we don't have that gas in the tank. There is no way we are going to make 11 miles, my wife is convinced we are, and she doesn't want to lose time by getting off the highway. It turns into a fight, I end up pulling off early to get gas.

Life is a choice, you can choose which gas trip is yours, the romantic experience under the stars or the nervous wreck, fighting and bickering until your tank runs out, both of you miserable.

Taking the time to fill up your tank before you leave, ensuring you have enough time to reach your destination, getting gas before your gas light turns on, or course correcting early instead of halfway through the drive, these are all small steps that have a monumental impact on your quality of life.

Take the time to identify what those emotional and financial checkpoints, determine how you will address them and course correct from them when they occur. Remember, you have already protected your worst-case scenario, and if you haven't then that is the correct the course you need.

A journey of 1000 miles, begins with a single step. One step in front of the other, don't look back, don't obsess over the details, just take that next step, and the next, and before you know it you will reach your destination.

Have confidence in your ability to course correct, to persevere, to adapt, and overcome life's challenges. You've made it this far in life, have faith that you will be able to make it the rest of the way.

Chapter 11

LIVING SUCCESS

I AM A FIRM BELIEVER that success is a unique experience. I believe what makes one successful will be different from person to person. Looking at others and following their recipes, step by step, is unlikely to produce good results. The circumstances that allowed your role model to succeed, may not apply to you, they may no longer be relevant, or they may not have worked the way your role model described.

As you come to the conclusion of this book, I want you to think about all the lessons you have learned and figure out how you can apply them to your life.

The key to financial and emotional happiness is to ingrain in yourself with the habits and thought patterns that bring about success. How those thought patterns and habits manifest for you, will be different. In this chapter, we are going to review the life lessons of this book, and we are going to discuss briefly how to turn theory into habit. Habits become part of who we are, part of our way of life, and will help us enjoy the rollercoaster ride, we call life.

Lesson #1: Emotions and Finance Go Hand-in-Hand

Making smart financial decisions, having confidence in those decisions - requires our emotional needs to be in line with our financial decisions. It requires that our emotional and physical needs be protected. This thought is embodied by phrases like "YOLO - You only live once" or "Living without Regrets."

Lesson #2: Know & Always Protect Your Bottom Line

Where is your line in the sand? What do you need in order to feel financially and emotionally secure? What will it take for you to feel confident in your ability to weather any storm life throws your way? How will you accumulate this wealth and freedom? There are no right or wrong answers. By protecting your bottom line, you give yourselves the confidence and breathing room to make smarter financial decisions.

P.S. Your needs, your line in the sand, will change with time - and your methods for meeting those needs should change as well.

Lesson #3: Where do you want to go in life?

Until you have clarity of where you want to go, what will it feel like once you are there? What will it look like, what are some of the stops you will have to make along the way? Until you have clarity, you will never be able to reach your destination. Once you have visualized your goal then you can increase your "luck surface area" and finally you are able to have a chance at making your dreams become a reality.

Lesson #4: Develop a Decision-Making Process

The most important lesson in this book is that you need a financial decision-making process. Your decision-making process, needs to be reflective of your emotional, physical, and financial needs. Until all your needs are in alignment, you will continually question your decisions. Does this decision bring me closer to my goals? What is my upside? Downside? What is my probability of success? Does this endanger my financial freedom? Is this worth the risk? The greater the clarity we have of our goals, the easier and quicker we can make these decisions. The more you practice *The 5-Minute Planning* Process the more it becomes part of who you are, and the more inline your decisions become. Better decisions means a happier and more fulfilling life.

Lesson #5: Life Is Filled with Hills and Valleys

Just when we think we've got a handle on life, it will throw us a curveball. Markets will tank, we will lose our job, our relationships struggle, and the list is literally endless in the ways that life will test us. We cannot predict life, what we can do is protect what is important to us, and "preserve, adapt and overcome." As life changes, so should our priorities, and our decisions. If we are continually course correcting, we stand a much better chance of succeeding than if we hang on with hope, and pray that life will turn out ok.

Lesson #6: A little know-how goes a long way

The only way you are going to know that you need to course correct is by having the knowledge and experience to identify events that signal a course correction. The more we learn about the world around us, the more we will be able to recognize when fundamental shifts are happening. This means reading newspapers, listening to experts, and forming our own opinions.

You will not always get it right, but if you have taken the time to get to know yourself, know your goals, and protect your emotional and financial wellbeing, then you should be able to weather any storm that life throws your way.

A great financial advisor can help you navigate this journey, they can act as your "subject matter expert", educating you about what you don't know, and pointing out the rapids over the horizon that we have not yet learned to spot. Of course, nobody is right 100% of the time, the trick is to be right more often than you are wrong, ensure that your mistakes are not fatal, and ensure you have a method to course correct and bring yourself back on track.

NEXT STEPS

CONGRATULATIONS, YOU HAVE COME to an end. I hope you found this book enlightening and helpful. Where do you go from here? The next step is to put this into practice in your life. You can do this on your own, or with your financial planner or advisor. If you do this with your planner, encourage them to read this book. I also teach advisor courses on how to implement these strategies.

If you choose to do this on your own, you may want to check out some of my upcoming books on:

- Investing
- Retirement
- Social Security Maximization

I also teach a hands-on workshop on these subjects; you can check them out at www.LeibelSternbach.com

If you have questions, feedback, suggestions, or just want to say hi, I love hearing from my readers and students. You can email me at Hello@LeibelSternbach.com.

Continue the conversion in our Facebook group *"The Financial Happiness Class"* @ https://www.facebook.com/groups/thefinancialhappinessclass

ABOUT LEIBEL STERNBACH

L EIBEL IS AN ACCREDITED Portfolio Management Advisor, an Enrolled Agent with the IRS, is a National Social Security Association Advisor certificate holder, and a Chartered Financial Consultant through The College of Financial Services. Leibel has passed his Series 65 and is a Life & Annuity Licenses holder and he has gone through the Ed Slott Elite IRA Advisor program.

Leibel's advice has been featured on Forbes, Investment-News, MarketWatch, LegalZoom, CNN, FOX, CBS, NBC, Readers Digest, USA Today, and Yahoo! Finance websites.

Leibel resides in Plainview, N.Y., with his wife, the midwife, Sammi Shmuela, and daughter, Liora. In his free time he teaches, cooks, writes, and reads anything he can get his hands on.

To learn more about Leibel Sternbach, visit his website LeibelSternbach.com or connect with him on LinkedIn